After the War on Drugs:
Blueprint for Regulation

TRANSFORM
DRUG POLICY FOUNDATION

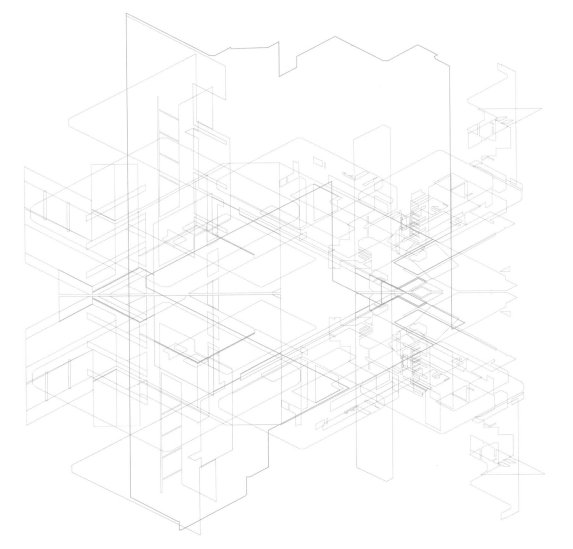

After the War on Drugs:
Blueprint for Regulation

For

Mo Mowlam

1949–2005

Minister responsible for UK Drug Policy 1999–2001

To celebrate her desire to tell the truth about drugs

"From my experience of being responsible for drugs policy... I came to the conclusion that legalisation and regulation of all drugs was the only way to reduce the harmful effects of this unstoppable activity."

The Guardian, 19 September 2002

Most of the referenced and further reading texts are available online—
see the PDF version at **www.tdpf.org.uk** for hyperlinks

Contents

Acknowledgements

Written by: Stephen Rolles

Contributing editors: Emily Crick, Mark Haden, Mike Jay, Danny Kushlick, Al Robertson

Thanks to: Damon Barrett, David Bewley-Taylor, Tom Blickman, Rielle Capler, Niamh Eastwood, Dale Gieringer, Ben Goldacre, Roger Goodman, Martin Jelsma, Rick Lines, Gillian Maxwell, Donald MacPherson, John Moore, Ethan Nadelmann, Lucy Platt, Frederick Polak, Lindsay Richardson, Sebastian Saville, Derek Williams, Alex Wodak and Martin Woodbridge

Also to: Martin Powell, Caroline Pringle and Jane Slater at Transform and Transform trustees, volunteers and supporters

Special thanks to: the J. Paul Getty Jr. Charitable Trust, and the Glass House Trust for supporting the production of this publication

Thanks to Transform's current and past funders including: the Esmée Fairbairn Foundation, the Allen Lane Foundation, the Linnet Trust, Atlantic Philanthropies, Ken Aylmer, Henry Hoare and individual donors

Foreword

Heroin, cocaine, ecstasy, cannabis, prescription and over-the-counter medicines, alcohol, tobacco, coffee, tea - we are all people who use drugs. Our refusal to acknowledge this comes from a deep-seated fear that *'we'* might become, or be seen as, one of *'them'*. What we really need to focus on is the difference between drug use and drug addiction or dependency. Global prohibitionist drug policy continues to focus efforts primarily on the substances alone. This is wrong.

Of course, the harms associated with some drugs are worse than others. Sometimes these are due to the degree of addictiveness of a particular drug. But most of the harms are due to the way that a particular drug is acquired (for example, in a dark alley versus from a pharmacy), the way in which it is used (as a pill, for example, versus smoking, snorting or injecting), and, even more importantly, the way in which society treats people who use drugs. The vast majority of the horrific harms associated with drug use—crime, HIV and other blood-borne infections, violence, incarceration, death—are clearly fuelled by the prohibitionist drug policies our governments pursue.

The use of non-medical drugs, and more importantly the *'War on Drugs'* itself, have had a profound influence on the global HIV epidemic over the past 25 years. Today, injecting drug use accounts for 30% of HIV infections worldwide outside of sub-Saharan Africa. In the Eastern Europe/Central Asia region as a whole over 60% of HIV infections are due to injecting drug use.

Global normative guidance on HIV prevention, treatment, care and support for people who inject drugs emphasises the use of a comprehensive set of evidence-based interventions aimed at reducing the harms associated with drug use. This normative guidance, as endorsed by the World Health Organization, the United Nations Joint Programme on HIV/AIDS, the International AIDS Society and other organisations, is in direct contrast to global drug control policy, as set out in the three major UN drug conventions of 1961, 1971 and 1988. These call for a strict prohibitionist stance on the production, distribution and use of non-medical drugs.

It doesn't take a rocket scientist to show that criminalising drugs and drug use has directly and indirectly led to a dramatic increase in drug-related harms, and that controlling and regulating the production and distribution of all drugs would go a long way towards reducing those harms. So long as we continue to define the drug user as *'other'* and define the drug itself as the problem, we will be trapped in our misguided and harm-inducing programmes and policies.

'After the War on Drugs: Blueprint for Regulation' lays out, for the first time, a set of practical and pragmatic options for a global regulatory system for non-medical drugs. It comes at a critical time. A number of Latin American governments, including Argentina, Brazil, Ecuador, Bolivia and Mexico have moved, or are moving, towards decriminalisation of drug possession and are shifting to a public health model to prevent and treat misuse of drugs. They are no longer able to tolerate the damage

done to their societies by the War on Drugs. Portugal decriminalised possession of all drugs in 2001. There are signs that the US government, under the new US 'Drug Czar' Gil Kerlikowske, is ready to review its position on the War on Drugs. Given that prohibitionist policy has been dominated by the US, and to some extent Russia, Japan and Sweden, any shifts in US policy could have dramatic effects at the global level.

This is not a radical book, nor does it posit radical approaches to global drug policy. In fact, as it points out, the prohibitionist model is the radical approach, in that it is based exclusively on a moral judgment against drug use and drug users and not on an evidence based approach to reducing drug-related harms. Underscoring a century of prohibitionist policy is a deep-seated fear that moving from prohibition to a regulatory approach will lead to a *'free-for-all'* situation *vis-à-vis* drug availability and use. *'Blueprint'* outlines clearly that this fear is irrational and that reform of any kind will be vastly superior to the status quo.

Reform will not happen overnight. In fact, as *'Blueprint'* makes clear, it will be important that changes are phased in gradually and closely monitored through intensive policy research that comprehensively documents health and other outcomes. The book proposes a number of regulatory options for each class of drug. Various approaches currently in use for the regulation and management of alcohol, tobacco, cannabis, and pharmaceutical medicines can be adapted for regulating non-medical drugs and drug use.

There often appears to be a vast gulf of irreconcilable differences between those of us advocating for harm reduction approaches to drug use, and those in the anti-drugs movement. To bridge the gap between these movements, harm reduction advocates must not be coy about the horrific problems that can be associated with drug use. Individuals in the anti-drugs movement are motivated too by their experience of these harms. Discussing these experiences openly and without prejudice could lead to a common language we can all share. If we are not able to reach out to the anti-drugs movement and find common ground, then our evidence will never overcome their fear. We must aim towards a unified voice where public health and human rights are two sides of the same coin.

'Blueprint' envisages a world in which non-medical drug supply and use is addressed through the right blend of compassion, pragmatism, and evidence-based interventions focussed on improving public health. These have been missing from the debate for too long. The time for change in global drug policy is long overdue. Nothing less than the future health of individuals, families, communities and societies is at stake.

Craig McClure

Former Executive Director, International AIDS Society

22 September 2009

Introduction

1.1   An ethics of effectiveness

Global drug policy is rooted in a laudable urge to address the very real harms that non-medical psychoactive drugs can create. Such concerns have driven a prohibitionist global agenda: an agenda that gives clear and direct moral authority to those who support it, while casting those who are against it as ethically and politically irresponsible. However, such binary thinking can be problematic. By defining the most stringent prohibition as the most moral position, it makes nuanced consideration of the impacts of prohibition difficult.

In particular, it makes it very difficult to look at and learn from the impacts and achievements of prohibition. Historic attempts to do so have foundered on a sense that analysing prohibition means questioning prohibition, and that questioning prohibition is in itself an immoral act—one that allies the questioner with the well known infamies of the world's illegal drug trade. Ironically, supporting the status quo perpetuates that trade, and the harms that it creates.

This is because uncritical support for the most stringent prohibition prevents policy makers and legislators from learning from experience. In fact, a century of experience with prohibition teaches that it can often be counter-productive; failing to reduce the harms it sets out to address as well as creating a raft of catastrophic unintended consequences. The extent of this failure has been chronicled in detail by many hundreds of sober, independent and objective assessments undertaken by government committees, academics, and Non Government Organisations across the world, over many decades.

It is not the purpose of this report to revisit these various findings; they are freely and easily available elsewhere.[1] Rather, we seek to reconsider the management of illicit drugs in the light of the experience that they represent and embody. Using that experience, we will set out a blueprint for non-medical drug management policies that will minimise the harms that such drug use creates, both on a personal and on a societal level.

In short, our goal is to define a set of practical and effective risk and harm management and reduction policies. Such policies will represent a clear and positive step towards the positive outcomes that prohibition has tried, and failed, to achieve. A strictly prohibitionist stance would understand them to be immoral, because they call for the legally regulated production and availability of many currently proscribed drugs. Transform's position is, in fact, driven by *an ethics of effectiveness*, and as such represent an attempt to re-frame the global harm management debate in exclusively practical terms.

Examples of inadequate regulation of currently legal drugs should not distract us from seeking more just and effective models for the regulation of currently illegal drugs. An ethics of effectiveness should be applied to all drugs. Indeed, historic failings in regulation of the tobacco and alcohol industries have more in common with the abrogation of control that prohibition exemplifies, than with best practice in regulation.

[1]   See Transform's collection of key reports www.tdpf.org.uk/Policy_KeyReports, and the Drug Policy Alliance online library /www.drugpolicy.org/library/.

1.2 No-one wants anarchy

Prohibition's emergence has been predicated on the concept of drugs as an existential *'threat'*, rather than a more conventionally conceived health or social policy issue. Prohibitionist rhetoric frames drugs as menacing not just health, but also our children, national security (*'our borders'*), or more broadly the moral fabric of society itself.

The prohibition paradigm is very much framed as a response to such threats, which has cast prohibitionist discourse as a moral crusade against an *'evil'* that threatens mankind itself. The preamble to the 1961 UN Single Convention on drugs, for example, establishes the context of the legal framework it has enshrined in these terms:

* *Concerned with the health and welfare of mankind*
* *Recognizing that addiction to narcotic drugs constitutes a serious evil for the individual and is fraught with social and economic danger to mankind*
* *Conscious of their duty to prevent and combat this evil*

Given this rhetorical context, it is easy to see how supporters of prohibition understand any kind of moves towards legal regulation of drug production and supply as being immoral, a form of surrender, or descent into anarchy. Criticism of more liberal drug policies is, in fact, often framed in these terms. Critics define one or more worst case scenarios, often extrapolated from *'what if?'* thinking built on an immediate and total absence of all drug control legislation, and then argue from the basis that such scenarios will be the norm.

It is important to note that, here, we agree with the prohibitionists. Full and immediate absence of all drug control infrastructure, disregarding all hard won harm and risk management experience, would lead to serious personal and social harms, outweighing any potential benefits. Ending prohibition on such terms would be both reckless and mistaken. Nobody wants anarchy, least of all us. This remains true whether it is criminal anarchy or entirely unfettered free markets. The need for the effective regulation of non-medical drug production and availability and use has always been, and remains, paramount.

> Instead of understanding drugs to be virulently, existentially threatening, we see them as creating issues that can be most helpfully defined in medical/health and social terms

Where we differ is on our sense of the function of regulation. Instead of understanding drugs to be virulently, existentially threatening, we see them as creating issues that can be most helpfully defined in medical/health and social terms. Drug using motivations and behaviours are many and varied, as are the outcomes of this use; they exist on a continuum from beneficial use, through non-problematic use, to problematic and chronic dependent use. Whilst this book emphasises the application of legal regulation where drug related harms are most evident, we also need to recognise that the majority of drug use is not significantly harmful, is an informed adult choice, and is rationally motivated—primarily by pleasure. So, rather than seeking to use statutory instruments to punish and eradicate moral evil, we look to help develop a clearly defined set of laws that will help local, national and global legislatures effectively manage the reality of the health and social issues we face, to the clearly definable, and measurable, benefit of all.

1.3   **Being radical?**

Supporters of prohibition present any steps towards legal regulation of drug markets as 'radical', and therefore innately confrontational and dangerous. However, the historical evidence demonstrates that, in fact, it is prohibition that is the radical policy. Legal regulation of drug production, supply and use is far more in line with currently accepted ways of managing health and social risks in almost all other spheres of life.

By contrast, the presentation of drugs as an existential *'threat'* has generated a policy response within which unevidenced and radical measures are justified. Drug policy has evolved within a context of *'securitization'*, characterised by increasing powers and resources for enforcement and state security apparatus. The outcomes of this strategy, framed as a drug *'war'*, include the legitimisation of propaganda, and the suspension of many of the working principles that define more conventional social policy, health or legal interventions. Given that the War on Drugs is predicated on *'eradication'* of the *'evil'* drug threat as a way of achieving a *'drug free world'*, it has effectively established a permanent state of war. This has led to a high level policy environment that ignores critical scientific thinking, and health and social policy norms. Fighting the threat becomes an end in itself and as such, it creates a largely self-referential and self-justifying rhetoric that makes meaningful evaluation, review and debate difficult, if not impossible.

Prohibition has become so entrenched and institutionalised that many in the drugs field, even those from the more critical progressive end of the spectrum, view it as immutable, an assumed reality of the legal and policy landscape to be worked within or around, rather than a policy choice. It is in this context that we seek to highlight how the basics of normative health and social policy can be applied to developing effective responses to drugs. Put bluntly, it is prohibition, not legal regulation that is the radical policy.

1.4   Our proposals

'Legalisation' is a process of legal reform only, regulation being the end point. So, when proponents of such moves are asked *'how would legalisation work?'*, or *'what would it look like?'* they can find it hard to give concrete responses. In the absence of more fully realised answers to these questions, myths and misunderstandings fill the void. Without a firm sense of what a post-legalisation world would look like, and how

market regulation could function, it is difficult for the discourse to move forward. This book aims to provide that foundation.

Thus, we are putting forward a set of proposals for how drug regulation might operate when the War on Drugs finally ends. In doing so, we have tried to create a very specific and practical set of suggestions for managing a variety of different drugs in ways appropriate to the individual effects that they have, and harms that they can cause. In particular, we have considered how such drugs could be produced and supplied, with the aim of taking back control of the drugs market from those least likely to manage it in a constructive way. We have based our thinking on currently existing models of controlled substance production, supply and management.

We begin this task by defining five models for regulating drug supply. We propose that drugs could be made available on prescription, through pharmacy sales, through sale from licensed outlets or venues, or even (in some admittedly rare cases) through sale from unlicensed suppliers. It should be noted that, under our proposals, this last is the exception, not the rule; and that, conversely, under prohibition, every single drug supplier is by definition unlicensed, and therefore beyond any form of constructive state or civil authority control or management.

Then, we look at the practical detail of regulation. We consider what kind of production and product controls could be put in place, to ensure that, for example, product strength and purity is safeguarded and consistent, and that appropriate product information is easily available to those using them. We define a range of supplier and outlet controls, and we balance that with some suggestions for purchaser and end user controls. Taken as a body, these will support and encourage drug users to use more moderately and responsibly, where appropriate in safer, more controlled environments. They are intended to minimise the personal and societal harms currently associated with drug taking. Again, under prohibition, harm minimisation of this type is rarely possible, nor generally even seen as desirable.

Of course, we accept that such changes will not come about overnight; nor should they. Legal regulation of production, supply and use represents a substantial realignment in drug management policy; like any such shift, it is not without risks, and so should be brought in slowly and carefully, with the impact of each incremental change carefully assessed before the next one is introduced. So, we propose a cautious, phased introduction. We look at ways of better assessing and ranking drug risks and harms to inform such decisions, and of managing appropriate legislation globally, nationally and locally. Effective policy needs effective research; we briefly lay out the terms of such research, and the goals it would need to achieve. Finally, moves towards legally regulated drug production and supply would have a wide range of broader social, political and economic impacts. We try to understand these, and look at ways of mitigating negative impacts whilst building on the positive.

By way of conclusion, we look at how regulated drug markets might work in practice. We begin with alcohol and tobacco. Despite their socially accepted status, they are capable of causing proven harms, and so their availability is carefully managed in most modern societies. We look at the most constructive ways of so doing, learning from historic mistakes. Then, we consider how regulated supply of cannabis, stimulants, psychedelics and depressants might work, based on the methods and processes defined in the preceding chapters.

The report is supplemented with two appendices. These give a broader context to the report, by describing the development and action of the current UN drug control system, and laying out current legal production frameworks for opium, coca, cannabis and pharmaceuticals.

1.5 **Knowing the limits**

It is crucial to recognise that legal regulation of drugs will not elimi-nate problematic drug use or dependence. Prohibition cannot produce a drug free world; regulatory models cannot produce a harm free world. Some individuals will continue to be harmed by their drug use, or as a result of the drug use of others. High-profile drug related tragedies will continue to make headlines. Legal regulation is no silver bullet or panacea for *the drug problem*, however it is conceived.

Legal regulation and control of drug markets can only seek to reduce or eliminate the harms that are created or exacerbated specifically by prohibition and illicit markets. It is also important to acknowledge that regulation of drug production is only one aspect of the broader drug policy debate. This wider field includes a range of intersecting arenas of policy thinking, including public health education and prevention, treatment and recovery, and the role of broader social policy concerns (including poverty, social exclusion, inequality, and human rights), and how they impact on drug use and drug markets.

Whilst these issues are not covered in any detail, a strong argument is made in these pages that prohibition creates both conceptual and practical obstacles to addressing the very real health concerns around problematic drug use. Its replacement with a regulatory system would enable, in terms of redirected resources, and empower, by reshaping the discourse and removing political and ideological obstacles, a public health and wellbeing based approach that would produce long term benefits. It would create a context that could facilitate tackling the social conditions that underlie problematic use, and better deal with wider drug related harms.

Regulation as envisaged here would also not entirely eliminate illicit drug markets and their associated problems, and it is important to note that any regulatory system is only as good as its enforcement. Clearly illicit activity continues to some extent with almost all commodities including drugs that are currently legal (alcohol, tobacco, and prescription drugs). Even a partial reduction in illicit markets and prohibition related harms still represents a huge net gain for society as a whole.

1.6 A starting point, not a conclusion

In publishing this book, we are not seeking to provide an exhaustive response to the practical issues surrounding legal regulation of drug production, supply and use. We have tried to demonstrate that legalisation and regulation do not mean anarchy; rather, plentiful drug management models already exist, and can be usefully and constructively applied to create a post-prohibition world, that learns from the mistakes of earlier drug management policies, and builds on their achievements.

However, we are very aware that this book is a starting point, not a conclusion. We do not seek to provide an unarguable answer to the problems of moving beyond prohibition; rather, we are looking to trigger debate and discussion about the most practical and constructive ways of achieving such a change. To facilitate this process we are launching various online discussion venues to accompany a series of discussion events, seminars and dialogues with key stakeholders. Message boards will allow readers to share their own opinions, while a *'wiki'* version of the report will allow reader expertise to be fed directly into an evolving future iteration of the book itself (visit **www.tdpf.org.uk** for more information).

We are also very aware that this book has been written from a specifically Western, and in particular European, point of view. We are in particular looking forward to input that will help broaden the book's perspective, and move it towards achieving a fully global awareness of the problems and solutions involved in moving towards a post-prohibition world.

Further reading

* *'After the War on Drugs: Options for Control'*, Transform Drug
  Policy Foundation, 2004
* *'After the War on Drugs: Tools for the Debate'*, Transform Drug
  Policy Foundation, 2006
* S. Rolles, *'Principles for rational drug policy making'*,
  (chapter in *'The Politics of Narcotic Drugs'*, Routledge, edited by
  J. Buxton, 2009)
* K. Grayson, *'Chasing Dragons—Security, Identity and Illicit Drugs in
  Canada'*, University of Toronto Press, 2008
* R. MacCoun, P. Reuter, *'Drug War Heresies: Learning from Other
  Vices, Times, & Places'*, Cambridge University Press, 2001

2

Five models for regulating drug supply

2.1   Regulation, prohibition and free markets

A spectrum of different approaches exists for controlling and regulating the production, supply and possession/use of different drugs. These can be broadly seen as existing on a continuum between the poles of completely unregulated free markets, and harshly enforced punitive prohibition. Ironically both of these extremes entail little or no market regulation. Between them sit the various options for legal regulation.

Prohibition/Criminalisation

Prohibiting/criminalising non-medical production, supply, possession and use, with punitive sanctions. Intensity of enforcement and severity of penalties can vary. Decriminalisation of personal possession and use can operate within a prohibitionist framework.[2]

EXAMPLE: heroin, cocaine, cannabis, ecstasy, etc.

MARKET CONTROLLER: criminal entrepreneurs, corrupt police and officials.

Regulated markets

A range of regulatory controls are deployed covering drug production and trade, product, gatekeepers of supply, and user. Some drugs, preparations, and activities remain prohibited.

EXAMPLE: prescription drugs, over the counter drugs, alcohol, tobacco.

MARKET CONTROLLER: moderate to intense regulation by government agencies.

Free market legalisation, or *'supermarket model'*

Drugs are legal and available for essentially unrestricted sale in the *'free market'*, like other consumer goods.

EXAMPLE: caffeinated drinks.

MARKET CONTROLLER: corporate/private enterprise, with minimal regulation by government agencies, voluntary codes for retailers.

2.1.1 Prohibition/criminalisation

Drug prohibition is a legal system under which the production, supply and use (or possession) of a list of specified drugs is proscribed by law and subject to punitive sanction. The overarching legal framework for global prohibition is defined by the three UN drug conventions

---

2 Either through policing practice (tolerance, *'turning a blind eye'*, de-prioritisation, non-enforcement, warnings/cautions etc.), or by changing responses to possession from criminal to civil or administrative sanctions. Access to drugs remains through illicit channels.

(see: *Appendix 1*, page 165) which frame domestic law across the globe. While these prohibitions are absolute in nature for all non-medical use, the detail of penalties and enforcement regimes are not specified and vary widely between states. The only legal production and supply models for drugs covered by the conventions are those permitted for medical and scientific purposes, such as opiates for maintenance prescribing for dependent users.[3] Some exemptions also operate in a legal grey area for traditional and religious uses (see: *5.5 Psychedelics*, page 146). Such models are consequently limited to a tiny proportion of the total using population.

Within the overarching global prohibition framework, individual states have considerable flexibility to determine enforcement regimes and punitive responses for prohibited activities. Indeed, responses to identical offences in different countries vary from *de facto* decriminalisation through to long prison sentences or, at the extremes, the death penalty. Trends in policy have diverged and polarised in recent years. While many countries' drug policies have become increasingly draconian and punitive,[4] there has been, throughout much of the developed world and in the newly industrialising countries of South America, a clear trend towards grudging tolerance and decriminalisation of drug possession and use.[5]

It is also important to note that, while exploration of these less punitive approaches to personal possession and use is allowed within the international legal framework, no form of legal production and supply of any drug prohibited under the conventions, or domestic law, can be explored for non-medical use *in any way*. The medical prescription model is the only real quasi-exception to this rigid rule; as such, it exists as an island of regulated production and supply, albeit within very narrow parameters. Beyond this there is zero flexibility for any

3   The conventions also control the medical uses of listed drugs, such as opiates for
    pain control.

4   *'At What Cost? HIV and Human Rights Consequences of the Global War on Drugs'*,
    International Harm Reduction Development Program, Open Society Institute, 2009.

5   *'Illicit drug use in the EU: legislative approaches'*, EMCDDA, 2005, and: T. Blickman,
    M. Jelsma, *'Drug Policy Reform in Practice'*, Transnational Institute, 2009.

17

regulated production and supply models to be piloted, tested, researched or explored. Furthermore, this absolute legal barrier creates genuine political obstacles to even discussing or proffering such policy alternatives. Defenders of the status quo often adopt dogmatic and entrenched moral positions, portraying regulatory legal alternatives as immoral, extreme, *'pro-drug'*,[6] radical, or even heretical. The clear implication is that debating such alternatives is a political *'no-go'* zone. Until relatively recently, the climate of fear thus created had pushed the law reform position to the margins of mainstream political discourse.

To the rational public health or social policy pragmatist, exploring and seeking out policy options that will deliver the best policy outcomes—an optimum point along this drug policy continuum—the idea that such an arbitrary barrier to policy research and development exists is difficult to justify.

This is especially true given that the vast majority of markets for goods and services, particularly ones that involve risk or potential harm (including many hundreds of medical and non-medical psychoactive drugs), are both legally available and regulated by governments.

> Legal regulation of potentially risky goods and activities is demonstrably not only the norm; it is one of the primary functions of government

A wide range of evidence based regulatory mechanisms and related enforcement/oversight agencies are deployed to control and manage producers, suppliers, environments, products and consumers. Legal regulation of potentially risky goods and activities is demonstrably not only the norm; it is one of the primary functions of government. For even the exploration of any such regulatory options to be forbidden in one, relatively narrow, field of human behaviour does not sit well with the wider commitment of the United Nations to *'promote social progress and better standards of life in larger freedom'*.[7]

---

6   UNODC executive director Antonio Costa has frequently used the term to describe advocates of legalisation/regulation.

7   The Universal Declaration of Human Rights, preamble.

2.1.2   **Regulated markets**

This book defines *'regulation'* as a set of legal rules and enforcement infrastructure designed to control or govern certain types of products and conduct—the various options being explored in detail in this and the following chapters. Activities that take place beyond the parameters of a given regulatory framework remain prohibited and subject to legal sanctions.

2.1.3   **Free market legalisation**

The free market model is often wrongly associated with the word *'legalisation'*, even deliberately so as the *'nightmare scenario'* promoted by opponents of reform, but is in reality only espoused by a very small group of hard core libertarian thinkers. With the possible exception of some very low risk products such as coffee or coca tea, such models are not appropriate for drugs, because they forgo the potential for most forms of responsible state intervention in market regulation and control. In this, they are handing control of drug markets to exploitative profiteers just as surely as prohibition.

Arguably such an approach[8] is, from a public health perspective at least, potentially an even worse scenario than unregulated criminal control of drug markets. Legal commercial actors—whose primary concern is profit maximisation—would be free to aggressively promote consumption through marketing and advertising.

The potential for such an approach to create unacceptable public health costs has been all too clearly demonstrated with the example of the free markets for tobacco in much of the developed world during the first 60 years of the 20th century, and to a greater extent in large parts of the developing world today (see: *5.1 Alcohol*, page 100, and *5.2 Tobacco*, page 105).

---

8   Nadelmann describes it as the *'supermarket model'* in a more detailed critique; see: E. Nadelmann *'Thinking Seriously About Alternatives to Drug Prohibition'*, Daedalus, 1992, 121: pages 87–132.

2.2   **Defining the five basic regulation models**

There are five basic models for regulating drug supply. We describe them below, starting with the most restrictive and moving to the most open. Variants on these models already exist and function across the world, supporting the entirely legal distribution of a range of medical, quasi-medical and non-medical psychoactive drugs.

Of course, the precise nature of the respective regulatory frameworks and enforcement infrastructure varies from country to country. There is also some degree of boundary blurring between these models. This leads to a certain amount of generalisation, but also helps emphasise that such models will inevitably operate differently in different locations.

We have also made some basic suggestions as to how to adapt these basic models to cater for the challenges of non-medical drug supply in the future.

2.3   **Prescription**

*   The prescription model is the most tightly controlled and enforced drug supply model currently in operation. Under this model, drugs are prescribed to a named user by a qualified and licensed medical practitioner. They are dispensed by a licensed practitioner or pharmacist from a licensed pharmacy or other designated outlet.

*   The process is controlled by a range of legislation, regulatory structures and enforcement bodies. These guide, oversee and police the prescribing doctors and dispensing pharmacists. They also help determine which drugs are available, in what form, where, and under what criteria.

* As the most tightly controlled and enforced supply model, the prescription model is the most expensive to administer. It is limited to medical necessity, which restricts its actual or potential use to the problematic/chronic dependent end of the drug use spectrum.[9] Most commonly, it supports maintenance prescribing as part of a treatment regimen or harm reduction programme. As such it will only ever involve a small fraction of the total drug using population, although it should be noted that this user group is disproportionately associated with the greatest personal and societal harms (especially under prohibition[10]).

* Substitute opiates such as methadone are the most commonly prescribed under such scenarios. Prescribed injectable heroin (diamorphine) also has a long history, and established evidence base.[11] Less common, although not unknown, is the prescription of stimulants, including amphetamines and cocaine.

* These long established models serve as an island of regulation for the very same drugs that are prohibited in all other scenarios. They provide a useful, if limited, demonstration of how legal regulation of drugs can help people become prescribed, rather than street, users; a clear example of the benefits of decriminalisation of drug use and regularisation of their supply route.

* This is particularly important given that such legal models have only evolved within generally hostile prohibition environments. As a rule, they have been minimally funded and politically unpopular. It is hard to know how such services would develop if managed with the latitude afforded to other, less controversial areas of patient care such as, for example, diabetes or mental health.

9   As well as, occasionally, for psycho-therapeutic uses of, for example, MDMA or certain hallucinogens. Cannabis prescribing is also somewhat different in practice.

10 See: discussion on disaggregating drug harms in *A Comparison of the Cost-effectiveness of the Prohibition and Regulation of Drugs*, Transform Drug Policy Foundation, 2009, (and *4.2 Assessing and ranking drug harms*, page 70).

11 G. Stimson, N. Metrebian, *'Prescribing heroin: what is the evidence?'*, Joseph Rowntree Foundation, 2003, and M. Ashton, J. Witton, *'Thematic review—heroin prescribing'*, Drug and Alcohol Findings, 2003, issue 9, page 16.

✻   Additional tiers of regulation have often been introduced within the basic prescribing model. These include requirements for consumption to be supervised in a specific venue, for very specific qualifying criteria to be met, or for the prescribing doctor to obtain a special licence. Prescribing is often time limited, administered in progressively reduced dosage, or made conditional on the patient meeting specific rehabilitation milestones.

✻   Some prescribing occurs in a grey area, where medical necessity has evolved into what is effectively maintained dependence. This is far more widespread, and includes dependence on various pain-killers (e.g. Vicodin, OxyContin) and tranquillisers (e.g. Valium).

✻   Maintenance prescribing for dependent users continues to create controversy within the field of medical ethics and practice. It raises some difficult questions for practitioners, as it exposes the grey areas between medical, quasi-medical and non-medical use. There are ongoing controversies and conflicts between the clear need to reduce harms associated with problematic illicit drug use and a reluctance to dispense drugs that are being used in any way non-medically.

✻   There are clear benefits of providing a safe and affordable supply of both drug and related paraphernalia. From a medical point of view, these are particularly helpful to those injecting, who are at high risk of contracting blood borne diseases. These benefits are sometimes undermined if practitioners are accused of supporting drug use for pleasure or recreation, while simultaneously 'failing to treat'—or even 'endorsing'—dependence.

✻   There appears to be a need for this field of care to evolve pragmatically to deal with modern challenges. Specialist training, a specific qualification/licence, or a new specialist prescribing-practitioner professional niche could be put in place. These would be supported by a strictly ethical code of conduct, and clearly defined general guidance. They would potentially be overseen by a new regulatory agency, or equivalent sub-group.

✳ Beyond this admittedly European perspective is an extensive, although poorly documented, history of opium registration systems in many Eastern and Middle Eastern countries. Users were registered and managed in Iran until 1953, and then again in the early 1970s (similar programmes are now being cautiously re-introduced); comparable systems also existed in Pakistan and India—where remnants still function—and in Bangladesh, Indonesia, Thailand and elsewhere.

2.4 Pharmacy model

✳ The pharmacy model, whilst still working within a clearly defined medical framework, is less restrictive and controlling than the prescription model. Pharmacists are trained and licensed to dispense prescriptions, although they cannot write them. They can also sell certain generally lower risk medical drugs from behind the counter. Such dispensing generally takes place from licensed pharmacy venues.

✳ Pharmacists are overseen by regulatory legislation, managed by various agencies and a clearly defined enforcement infrastructure. They either fulfil prescriptions, or sell over the counter products. Access to the latter is only possible if firm, non-negotiable criteria are met. These include restrictions according to buyer age, level of intoxication, quantity requested, or case-specific concerns relating to potential misuse. In addition, pharmacists are trained to offer basic medical advice, support and information.

✳ In some places, pharmacists are already involved in drug

management regimes. For example, in the UK, they are required to supervise the on-site consumption of some maintenance methadone prescriptions—a precaution against diversion to the illicit market.

* The existing pharmacy model is not directly involved in dispensing or vending drugs for non-medical use. However, it could easily be adapted and developed into an effective way of managing the availability of currently illicit drugs for such purposes. Licensed and trained professionals could serve as gatekeepers for a range of such drugs. They would be legally required to restrict sales according to the kind of strict criteria defined above, and would also act as a source of realistic, well informed and practical advice and support.

* A specialist, non-medical drug pharmacist would occupy a distinct professional niche, one that would need careful development, definition and management. This new role would be subject to a similar code of practice to that of more conventional pharmacists, but with additional access control criteria. These specialist pharmacists would also be required to offer advice about harm reduction, safer use, and treatment services and referrals to help users quit, where appropriate. Such advice would be supported by necessary additional training or experience in drug counselling. They could either operate alongside existing pharmacies (subject to appropriate licensing conditions) or from separate licensed outlets.

2.5 Licensed sales

* Current best practice in licensed sales of alcohol and tobacco offers a less restrictive, more flexible infrastructure for the licensed sales of certain lower risk non-medical drugs (see: *5.1 Alcohol*, page 100, and *5.2 Tobacco*, page 105). Such a system would put various combinations of regulatory controls in place to manage the vendor, the

supply outlet, the product and the purchaser, as appropriate.

✻ Much like current best practice in alcohol and tobacco management programmes, a raft of centrally determined framework policy and regulatory legislation would be put in place. This would be overseen and enforced by municipal, regional or national authorities, according to local legal and cultural norms. These authorities would act as the licensing body, and would be able to tailor the regulatory framework to local needs and policy priorities. They would be supported by police, customs, trading standards, and health and safety infrastructure, as appropriate.

✻ As noted in the pharmacy model above, licence holders could be required to offer advice about harm reduction, safer use, and treatment services, where appropriate. They might also be required to undergo necessary additional training in drug counselling, or to have pre-existing drug counselling experience.

2.6 Licensed premises

✻ Public houses and bars serving alcohol offer the most common example of premises licensed for sale and consumption. Under this long established system, various controls exist over the venue and (in particular) the licensee. He or she is responsible for restricting sales on the basis of age, intoxication and hours of opening.

✻ The licensing authority is usually a tier of local government, which manages and enforces a series of centrally determined regulations. A clearly defined hierarchy of sanctions for licence infringements includes a sliding scale of fines, loss of licence, and even criminal penalties. Licensees can also be held partially or wholly liable for how their customers behave—punishable examples include anti-social behaviour, noise, littering and drink driving.

*   The cannabis *'coffee shop'* system in the Netherlands offers another useful example of premises licensed to sell more contentious products (see: *5.3 Cannabis*, page 110). Through these coffee shops, the Dutch authorities have gone some way towards legally licensing the sale and consumption of cannabis. However, it should be noted that, even here, the cannabis trade is not subject to full legal regulation; supply to the coffee shops remains illicit, even though low level supply and consumption within them is tolerated. The coffee shops themselves operate under a range of strict—and strictly policed—conditions.

*   Supervised venues for the dispensing and consumption of prescribed diamorphine (heroin) are another form of licensed venue. They are subject to strict licensing, regular external scrutiny and firm enforcement, although they only provide drugs on a prescription basis.

*   Lessons can also be learned from licensing and regulating regimes put in place to manage other restricted (and potentially harmful) activities including gambling, certain kinds of entertainment, and sex work.[12]

*   The examples given above suggest that a functioning licensed premises for drugs would remain relatively restricted in terms of how it offered drugs, and who it offered them to. Given this, it could combine elements of existing licensed premises, licensed sales, and specialist pharmacy models, to ensure that moderate drug use took place in a safer, more supportive environment.

2.7   Unlicensed sales

*   Certain psychoactive substances deemed sufficiently low risk, such as coffee, traditional use of coca tea and some low strength

---

12 R. MacCoun, P. Reuter, *'Drug War Heresies: Learning from Other Vices, Times, & Places'*, Cambridge University Press, 2001.

painkillers, are subject to little or no licensing. Here, regulation focuses on standard product descriptions and labelling. Where appropriate, food and beverage legislation (dealing with packaging, sell by dates, ingredients etc.) comes into play. These substances are effectively freely available, although they may in some cases be subject to certain localised restrictions or voluntary codes.

Regulated Market Model

There has been much recent discussion responding to the historic public health failings of tobacco policy (see: *5.2 Tobacco*, page 105). This has generated proposals for a new regulatory model that could also be applied to other drugs. Professor Ron Borland has proposed the Regulated Market Model (RMM), which is built on the assumption that smoked tobacco is not an ordinary consumer product.

Even when used as directed, tobacco is both highly addictive and significantly harmful to personal health. It follows that any commercial marketing, which aims to increase tobacco consumption and thus profitability, will inevitability lead to unacceptable increases in health harms.

Responding to this, the proposed model would maintain legal access to adults but remove incentives for profit motivated efforts to increase consumption by creating even more addictive products, by increasing usage of existing products, or by encouraging new consumers to begin smoking. It would establish a regulatory agency (a Tobacco Products Agency, or TPA) to act as the bridge between manufacturers and retailers.

The TPA would take complete control over the product and all related marketing activity, managing tobacco product type, production, packaging and marketing. Competitive commercial interaction would still occur at point of production, and point of supply. Tobacco producers would compete to supply the TPA with raw materials, while retailers would profit from selling tobacco products to appropriate customers.

The TPA would thus be able to pursue public health goals by managing and possibly even reducing consumption, instead of profit goals by actively working to maximise tobacco usage.[13] (See graphic overleaf)

13　R. Borland, '*A strategy for controlling the marketing of tobacco products: a regulated market model*', Tobacco Control, 2003, Vol. 12, page 377.

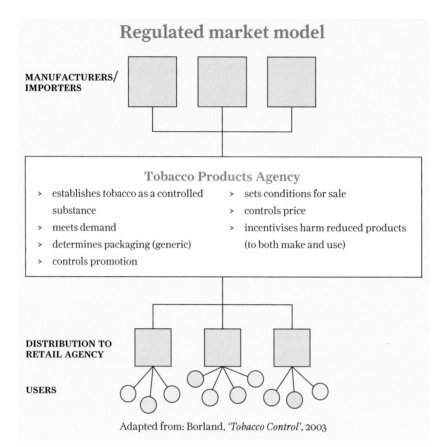

Regulated market model

**MANUFACTURERS/
IMPORTERS**

Tobacco Products Agency

> establishes tobacco as a controlled
  substance
> meets demand
> determines packaging (generic)
> controls promotion

> sets conditions for sale
> controls price
> incentivises harm reduced products
  (to both make and use)

**DISTRIBUTION TO
RETAIL AGENCY**

USERS

Adapted from: Borland, *'Tobacco Control'*, 2003

The practical detail of regulation

3.1   **Production controls**

Surprisingly, the problems of regulating drug production require far less discussion than the problems of drug supply regulation. There are already a large number of well established businesses engaged in the production of plant-based and synthetic psychoactive drugs. They are doing so entirely within existing regional, national, and global legal frameworks.

Given this, drug production for non-medical use will mostly require expansion of existing frameworks, rather than development of new ones. We demonstrate this with the following summary of existing legal and regulated production of opium/heroin, coca/cocaine, and cannabis. For a more detailed discussion of current legal drug production summarised below; see: *Appendix 2*, page 193.

It should also be noted that establishing a legal regime permitting the sale and consumption of drugs for non-medical use would allow these legally regulated companies to compete directly with current, illegal non-medical drug providers. The relative quality and legality of their products, over and above any price advantage they would have, would no doubt allow them to take very substantial market share from their criminal competitors as their market presence grows.

There are economic and social issues to be addressed in any transition from criminal to legally regulated system; for example, it would raise important development issues in previous illicit drug producing areas (see: *4.5 Broader social, political and economic impacts*, page 84). In the long run, however, stripping a wide range of international criminal organisations of one of their central profit streams can only be regarded as a positive outcome.

3.1.1 Current legal production: opiates, cocaine, cannabis, pharmaceuticals

i Legal opium/opiate production

Almost half[14] of global opium is legally produced for processing into various opiate based medicines. Any country can formally apply to the UN's Commission on Narcotic Drugs to cultivate, produce and trade in licit opium, under the auspices of the UN Single Convention on Narcotics Drugs 1961 and under the supervision and guidance of the International Narcotic Control Board (INCB). As of 2001 there were eighteen countries that do, including Australia, Turkey, India, China and the UK.

The international licensing control system seeks to permit and regulate legitimate production and use, and at the same time prevent diversion to the illicit market for non-medical use. National governments deal with the licensing and inspection of cultivation, production, manufacture and trade in the controlled substances whilst being monitored by the INCB, which is the UN body responsible for ensuring a balance between legitimate production and legitimate requirements.

---

14 Licit opium production accounted for more than half of global opium production until around 2005-6, and the subsequent bumper harvests of illicit opium in Afghanistan.

Expanded production of opium and derived products under existing frameworks is clearly both feasible and non-problematic. Even with the economic pressures from illicit demand as they currently exist, the legal production and transit of both raw opium and processed opiate pharmaceutical products currently takes place on a large scale without significant security or diversion issues.

It is likely that the expansion of legally regulated opiate use would initially take place within existing medical prescription models; indeed, this process is already underway, albeit slowly. More significant shifts from illicit to licit production (be it via more substantial expansion of prescribing models, or some other appropriate form of licensed sales), would take place incrementally over a number of years.

This would allow for a manageable transition period during which the relevant regulatory and enforcement infrastructure could be developed or expanded. Any emerging challenges could be responded to as and when they came up. As this phased process continues, demand for illicit product will correspondingly diminish, and with it the economic incentives for diversion or illicit production to occur.

As noted above, such a change is a mixed blessing for some. In this case, it raises potentially significant development issues for Afghanistan, which currently produces an estimated 93% of the world's illicit opium, contributing over half of its GDP.[15] Any shift away from opium production as a key source of income would have to be carefully managed, especially in such a sensitive area (see: *4.5 Broader social, political and economic impacts*, page 84).

ii **Legal coca/cocaine production**

Both the coca leaf and its active drug content cocaine, are subject to strict controls under the 1961 UN Single Convention on Narcotic Drugs,

---

15 *'In Afghanistan, the total export value of opium and heroin being trafficked to neighbouring countries in 2007 is $US 4 billion, an increase of 29% over 2006. That means that opium now accounts for more than half (53%) of the country's licit GDP.'*
'Afghanistan: Opium Survey 2007', UNODC, 2007, page iii.

in a similar fashion to opium and opium-based pharmaceuticals. Legal production of both does take place, but on a much smaller scale than permitted opium production.

Legal production of coca in the Andean region continues for use as a beverage flavouring (mostly for Coca-Cola), the leaf being exported to the US where it is *'de-cocainised'* by a pharmaceutical company licensed by the federal Drug Enforcement Agency. The extracted cocaine is used as an anaesthetic medicine around the world.

Various low potency coca products, including the coca leaf itself, coca tea, and coca based foods and traditional medicines, are also common in this part of the world. They exist in a legal grey area, and remain the subject of ongoing wrangling between the UN drug agencies and Bolivia and Peru.

Given all this, legal coca production for use in its raw leaf form, in lightly processed products, or as pharmaceutical cocaine, demonstrably does not present any significant problems in and of itself. When assessed from the point of view of potential health harms caused, low potency coca products (leaf and tea) do not require any more controls than equivalent products such as coffee. The processing of coca into pharmaceutical cocaine would take place at an industrial level for which any security and product regulation issues would operate within well established models.

The key problems in any such system are the ones already seen in coca producing regions: the destabilising economic tensions and social harms created by any parallel illicit markets. Regulating legal production of coca leaf in line with the established fair trade guidelines—price guarantees along with a range of other social and

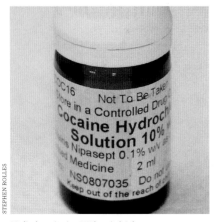

STEPHEN ROLLES

Medical cocaine in a UK hospital, July 2009

environmental protections (for growers of coffee, cocoa, sugar, etc.)—
would go some way to ameliorating these problems. Furthermore, in a
similar fashion to opium and cannabis, such problems would progressively diminish with the shrinking demand for illicit supply, as the
global market shifted towards legal regulation.

Specific trade and development issues might arise during this transition period, including the potential for the UN drug agencies to license
production of coca to a limited number of countries (for example
limiting it to Andean nations), or for individual states to begin to cultivate coca for their domestic markets (see: *4.5 Broader social, political and
economic impacts*, page 84).

iii **Legal cannabis production**

Cannabis has been produced in a number of different countries, notably
the US and Canada, over a number of decades, primarily for various
medical uses and preparations. Some has been grown under licence or
by the state, some by quasi-legal or tolerated patient co-ops.

This has created a significant body of experience concerning legal regulation of cannabis production. It also demonstrates how production
can take place in a way that addresses security concerns and quality
control issues. Taken together, these will provide clear guidance for
the development of a functioning model for commercial non-medical
production in the future.

Legitimate concerns about diversion to illegal markets could be
addressed through appropriate licensing of growers and suppliers
combined with effective enforcement where violations of licensing
conditions were identified. Economic incentives to divert to illegal
markets would progressively diminish as legal production expanded
and undermined the profits currently on offer to illegal suppliers.

Economic incentives to divert to illegal markets would progressively diminish as legal production expanded and undermined the profits currently on offer to illegal suppliers

As with opium and coca products, the expansion of legal production would be incremental over a number of years. This would allow for a manageable transition, and in particular the evolution of an effective regulatory infrastructure in response to any emerging issues and challenges.

Making a reliable retail supply of cannabis available would also impact substantially on home growing for personal use. It would become an increasingly minority pursuit, the preserve of a small group of hobbyists or connoisseurs—rather like home brewing of wine or beer. Basic guidelines could be issued and limits placed on how much production was allowed for any individual, but experience with such schemes in Europe suggests they are hard to enforce and often ignored by police and growers alike.

A licensing model might become appropriate for small to medium sized cannabis clubs or societies of growers who share/supply/exchange on a non-profit basis, so that age and quality controls could be put in place, and some degree of accountability could be established. Of course, it could be that there would be little to no interest in home growing; home tobacco growing in the UK—theoretically subject to customs duty—is virtually non-existent.

For a more detailed discussion of current legal drug production summarised above, see: *Appendix 2*, page 193.

iv   **Legal pharmaceutical production**

Existing models for production of many thousands of pharmaceutical drugs already exist. They are built round very strict regulation, particularly of quality control, security, and transit issues. Given that (as highlighted with cocaine and opiates) many legal pharmaceuticals are the same drugs as those used non-medically, little or no change would be required here.

Established models would be more than adequate to support licensed expansion of production for non-medical use. Indeed, once again, security and diversion issues would become less pressing over time.

3.2 Availability controls

Minimising the harm that a given drug creates, both to users and the broader society that he or she is a part of, is a key motivation of any drug control regime. It seems logical, therefore, that the best way to minimise such harms is by limiting the availability of the drug that causes them, and thus minimising use—the key goal of supply side drug prohibition and enforcement.

However, accurate measurements of illicit drug availability are difficult to come by, and so the relative success or failure of such regimes is hard to judge. Moreover, limiting legal availability of a given drug can—counter-intuitively—increase rather than decrease the harms that it creates, by gifting its distribution and sale into the hands of criminal profiteers and cultures that have no interest in serving the broader social good.

Reducing availability is often stated as a primary policy goal[16] but, remarkably, the concept of availability has been very poorly explored and expressed. Almost no data is systematically collected on drug availability anywhere, beyond inference from price and purity data, occasionally through user surveys, or more commonly via meaningless proxy measures, such as levels of drug seizures. Even if such data were to be gathered, the mostly covert and informal nature of the illicit drug trade would make it very difficult to achieve a reliable overview of drug availability. From the limited data we do have the clear inference is that illicit drug availability has more than kept pace with demand—indeed

---

16 See example (UK) in *'After the War on Drugs: Options for Control'*, Transform Drug Policy Foundation, 2005, page 24.

availability is generally acknowledged to have been increasing despite the growing resources directed into supply side enforcement.

Unlike illicit availability, legal product availability, in its various forms, can be very precisely measured and controlled. This can be managed through the nature and intensity of regulatory controls deployed and the strictness of, and resources directed towards, their enforcement. Policy can thus be adapted to different or changing policy priorities, or changes in public mood. At a practical level, policy can evolve according to the needs of different environments, and respond swiftly to changing circumstances and emerging challenges.

Some readers may baulk at the restrictive and intrusive nature of some of the regulations outlined below. It is the aim of this book to show that a range of options is available to control production, supply and use in a legally regulated regime. It is the more or less democratic will of the people affected that will determine the fine tuning of restrictions as applied in any given scenario. However, it is to be assumed that more restrictive regimes would be applied in the initial phase of legal regulation, with a view to lightening the regulatory touch further down the line, guided by evidence of its effectiveness, and as more positive social norms and controls evolved (see: *4.1 A cautious, phased introduction*, page 67).

One of the many harms created by a blanket prohibition is the reduction in the range of choice of drugs available to consumers. The consequence of an illicit market governed almost exclusively by the need to maximise profits, is that it becomes increasingly dominated by the more concentrated, potent and risky drug products and preparations that offer the greatest profits—injected heroin, crack cocaine, and methamphetamine for example. When control by criminal profiteers is replaced with a legal regime controlled by public health and state authorities, we would expect that much lower strength versions of drugs would be more widely available. There is plenty of evidence, especially from the alcohol field, to demonstrate that most users rationally tend to choose milder versions. Emerging regulatory approaches have the flexibility and options for control to take account of the wider range of drugs available.

A crucial point to emphasise is, therefore, that public management of drug availability ensures that regulatory models and additional controls can be deployed differentially, at different levels of intensity, depending on the risks of a given product or activity. It is not just that the greater risks associated with a given drug and/or population of users (or potential users) justifies greater regulation on practical risk reduction grounds, but that the differential application of regulatory controls can create an availability gradient that corresponds to the risk gradient of different drugs/preparations, behaviours and environments in which they are consumed.

This availability/risk gradient can support broader public health and harm reduction goals by progressively discouraging higher risk products, preparations and behaviours, and *'nudging'* patterns of use towards less risky products, preparations and behaviours, and in the longer term fostering social norms around more responsible and less harmful use. As already touched upon, illicit drug culture is not neutral in this regard; in many instances it actively pushes use in the opposite direction, towards increasingly harmful products, preparations, behaviours and environments (see, for example, discussion of coca and cocaine products in *5.4 Stimulants*, page 117).

Prohibition—and the illicit drug markets and cultures it has fostered—undermines social norms and controls that can encourage more responsible drug using decisions and discourage more harmful or risky ones. This process is a counterintuitive one. Punitive prohibitions are clearly intended to achieve precisely the opposite. What is now evident from the experience of the past half century or more is that prohibition, when used as a tool for public health education and improvement, fails in this goal. This failure occurs because prohibition cedes control of drug availability to those least qualified or incentivised to manage it responsibly, motivated solely by profit maximisation.

The key point to emphasise is that regulated availability affords the opportunity for control which is absent under prohibition. Controlled availability does not automatically translate into increased availability. Rather than the one size fits all approach of prohibition, legal regulation creates opportunities for nuance and flexibility through differential application along a range of policy vectors. That flexibility will help policy makers balance the need to regulate current, prohibition-driven patterns of use in the short term, with longer term policies that will encourage new lower-risk patterns of use.

With legal regulation and management of currently illicit drugs, the opportunity exists not only to arrest this general trend towards harm maximisation created by prohibition, but to begin to reverse it and in the medium to long term, move decisively in the opposite direction.

3.3 Product controls

3.3.1 Dosage, preparation controls

As discussed elsewhere (see: *4.2 Assessing and ranking drug harms*, page 70.), risks associated with a given drug are significantly determined by the nature of the drug preparation, the dosage, and the consumption method.

Drugs that come in pill or powder form should be made available in standardised units. Such standardisation ensures that the amount being consumed is clearly understood. It also allows information associated with the product to be related clearly and directly to those units. The dosage for a standardised unit should be determined by the toxic/dose risk profile of the drug in question.

The availability of particular preparations of each drug, and the levels of control exercised over each preparation, will need to be determined on a case by case basis. In general, weaker, slower release oral preparations should be more easily available. Stronger, more rapid release versions should be more difficult to come by. The highest risk preparations, particularly if for use via injecting, should only be accessible on the most restrictive terms—usually either on prescription, or for supervised use.

The risk of diversion into secondary, illicit markets could be mitigated through the use of microtaggants. These are microscopic tracers that function like a chemical barcode, and can be added to pharmaceutical drug preparations. They would help the licensing authorities identify and take action against the source—perhaps the drug's named user or original supplier—of any illicit secondary sales.

3.3.2 **Price controls**

Price controls are highly flexible and can potentially be targeted at specific products, populations of users, types of outlets or geographical regions associated with particular concerns

Legal regulation allows the government to influence drug prices, either through taxation added (or subsidy provided) to a market determined price, or though more direct price fixing interventions. Taxation could be set either on a fixed tax per unit basis, or as a percentage of goods/services supplied (as, for example, VAT is currently set). Depending on how they are set, price controls could either lead to tax revenue generation, or demand state subsidy of drug products.

Optimum drug pricing can be summarised as creating a balance between two conflicting needs. Prices should at once be sufficiently high to discourage misuse, and sufficiently low to ensure that under-cutting them is not profitable for illicit drug suppliers.

Of course, this is a very simple presentation of the problem. Caution needs to be exercised when making generalisations about the impacts that price management can have. It should be noted that price adjustments potentially have very different impacts on different sub-populations of users, and on different markets for different drugs. Wide variations in price elasticity of demand—that is, the degree to which demand responds to changes in price—have been observed in different groups of drug users, drugs, and patterns of use.

For example, increasing price does not always reduce levels of consumption (or *vice versa*). Despite the fact that such a price-driven reduction is both a fundamental tenet of micro economics, and demonstrable with some drugs and related user populations (e.g. alcohol and tobacco), patterns of use demonstrably often rise and fall independently of price. In the US, to take one example, the price of cocaine has dropped by 80% over the last 25 years, but consumption has fallen.

The price levels for legally supplied drugs (inclusive of any government interventions) will naturally have an impact on the size of any parallel illicit market, the key factor being the relative price difference. It is the huge profit margins offered by the current illegal market—with supply side enforcement somewhat counter-intuitively acting as an informal price support system—that exert the powerful attraction to the criminal organisations and individuals.

Assuming market prices for some key drugs would fall (most obvi-ously for heroin and cocaine), and as consumption progressively shifts to licit supply, so we can expect an associated fall in the size of illicit profit opportunity on offer, the incentive for criminal involvement on a per unit basis, and a corresponding fall in the level and intensity of violence associated with the illicit market. The ability and incentive of illicit traders to undercut the licit market will diminish as price approaches the licit market production cost price and potential profit margins shrink.

This all points to a need for careful, realistic, case by case management of drug pricing levels. If so managed, changes in drug price point can be managed to have maximum impact on levels of use, levels of illicit supply activity, levels of crime committed by users fundraising to buy drugs, and levels of taxation revenue generated. Setting an optimum price for a given product, in a particular environment, will require careful balancing of these various impacts, which are often in conflict with each other. This is a challenge familiar to policy makers who have managed pricing controls for alcohol and tobacco; there are many useful lessons to be learned from their experience in this field.

General drug pricing considerations include:

* The economic burden of drug expenditure relative to total disposable income of the user is a key factor. If initial prices are sufficiently low and/or if use is moderate/occasional, total spend is likely to be low and even a dramatic change in price is unlikely to have much impact on demand. Conversely, where use is frequent and total spend relative to disposable income is high, price changes can have significant impacts on levels of use (e.g. alcohol and tobacco).

* Those with lower disposable incomes—significantly including young people—will generally be more susceptible to price controls intended to moderate levels of consumption. It should however be borne in mind that, although such increases can have a positive impact on young people (alcohol research for example shows price increases are linked to reduced use), the broader socio-economic/class impact of price control policies can raise contentious issues.

✼　　A general assumption is that a dependent user's need to maintain their habit makes their demand less price elastic than other consumers. Increased price may have unintended consequences amongst those with low disposable incomes, such as fundraising-related offending (often observed with illicit cocaine and heroin users), or reduced spending on, for example, healthy diet (also observed with dependent alcohol and tobacco users).

✼　　Availability and costs of substitute drugs, or substitute recreational activities, is also a factor in determining the impact of pricing changes on drug use. Increasing the price of one drug may divert users to cheaper alternatives. The impacts of such displacement are potentially either positive or negative, depending on exactly what the replacement drug or activity is. Displacement can also take place towards riskier but more cost-effective methods of administration, such as injecting. Of course, it should also be noted that policy-making can attempt to encourage positive displacement (see below).

User choice of licit or illicit supply will be determined by a complex interplay of variables, not just relative prices, making generalisations difficult. Future pricing policy decisions will have to be based on the cautious testing of different pricing regimes and their impacts on various indicators amongst different populations—an ongoing system for outcome evaluation necessarily built into any regulatory infrastructure.

Interventions on price are a particularly useful policy tool, as once a price control infrastructure is established it allows for relatively rapid responses to changing circumstances and emerging problems. Price controls are highly flexible and can potentially be targeted at specific products, populations of users, types of outlets or geographical regions associated with particular concerns. Differential application of such price controls can also contribute to an incentive-disincentive gradient that can help encourage more responsible using behaviours and the use of lower risk products.

Whilst there is a need to be cautious in generalising between drugs, the range of experiences with alcohol and tobacco policy provides a useful starting point to inform drug pricing policy more generally. As well as demonstrating where policy may be effective it needs to be acknowledged that political issues continue to cloud government price interventions on both of these drugs; the potential to generate substantial tax revenue may negatively impact on government public health priorities (which would generally aim to moderate use and thus reduce revenue), whilst the public unpopularity of increasing taxes, the lobbying power of the production and supply industries, and employment of potential voters within the respective production and supply industries are also important political considerations.

The occasionally mooted idea that tax revenue from drugs could be redirected into drug services (prevention, education and treatment/recovery) is one that has a certain populist appeal, but is not useful beyond the broadest of cost benefit considerations. Service provision should be determined by need and evidence of efficacy, not by the whims of tax revenue generation.

3.3.3 Packaging controls

i Tamper proofing

Established product packaging types used for pharmaceutical drugs and some food products can reduce the possibilities for tampering with drugs, and allow the purchaser/user to know if tampering has occurred. Examples include blister packs, sealed ampoules, and other forms of sealed containers, such as *'pop top'* lids on foods.

ii   **Child proofing**

Established childproof containers (as used for medicines) should be used as a default for all licensed psychoactive substances. Where appropriate an additional requirement could be made for commercial or domestic storage in sealed/locked cabinets.

iii   **Information on packaging**

Information on packaging should be based on established norms for pharmaceutical drugs—with additional information and messages as appropriate. Contents and prominence of packaging information should be determined by the appropriate public health authority and be legally enforced. Information should include:

* **Contents**: clearly stated—both technical names and terms in popular usage.
* **Dosage**: total contents and contents per unit (e.g. pill) where appropriate.
* **Effects and side effects—positive and negative**: at different dosages (including likely different effects on different users; e.g. body-mass).
* **General risks**: acute and chronic toxicity, dependence—and danger signs.
* **Specific risks**: re; pregnancy, certain medical conditions (e.g. heart problems, diabetes, mental health).
* **Secondary risks**: impaired driving/operating machinery/workplace competence.
* **Harm reduction**: how to minimise risk.
* **Contraindications**: risks of poly-drug use: both with regards to other non-medical use or use with prescribed/non-prescribed medications.

❋ **Where to find more information/support services**: help lines, websites etc.

❋ **Legal disclaimer**: producer/vendor liability: *'Consumption is at the risk of user'*, *'Not for medical use'*, *'Consumption for Over 18s only'*, *'Consumption only for named purchaser'*, etc.

❋ **Anti-counterfeiting measures** (if required): holograms etc., as seen with tax stamps on some alcohol products.

❋ **Use-by dates**.

These guidelines apply for offsite sale or supply, and will need some level of flexibility. For example, following the model of some prescription or over the counter drugs, certain product and packaging formats might demand a summary of key information, or a single prominent warning, on one packaging component (e.g. the pill blister-pack). This would be supported by a paper insert giving more detailed product information. Where drugs are supplied for on-site use, supervised use, or use by licensed individuals, different regulations may apply, including on-site, clearly visible provision of the relevant information. This would not necessarily be available on the product itself, which may be provided without packaging in some scenarios.

iv   **No on-pack branding or marketing communications**

In line with the wider controls on all forms of advertising, marketing and promotion, no branded or more general marketing communications should be permitted on any psychoactive drug packaging. The resultant packs would be modelled on current medical drug packaging, or plain packaging models proposed for tobacco.[17] Clear guidelines for such controls should be mandated by the appropriate public health authority and enforced by the relevant authorities as part of licensing conditions. These authorities should also define and manage any on- or in-pack health and safety messaging.

---

[17]   R. Cunningham, *'Smoke and Mirrors: The Canadian Tobacco War'*, IDRC, 1996, chapter 12: *'Plain Packaging'*.

v   **Named user purchaser identification**

In some scenarios, such as under a licensed purchaser model (see below) it may be appropriate to record a named user on the packaging. This could be managed through print, digital tagging or bar-codes, or through some combination of all three. It would emphasise that the product is for use by the named individual only, and that they are directly responsible for it and its use. Product tagging could be linked to sanctions, such as loss of purchaser licence, if the product ends up in the hands of a third party.

3.4   Supplier and outlet controls

The licensing of an individual or corporate vendor/supplier can be linked to some or all of the conditions listed here. Licensed individuals or companies could be subject to a hierarchy of penalties for violations, including fines, loss of licence, or other appropriate civil or criminal sanctions. As described above, in *chapter 2, Five models for regulating drug supply*, requirements for individual vendors to have specialist training, and/or experience, and abide by a legally mandated code of conduct, can be threaded through all licensed sales models.

3.4.1   Advertising/marketing controls

STANFORD SCHOOL OF MEDICINE

Unacceptable drug marketing: 1950s cigarette advertising

Links between the advertising and promotion of alcohol and tobacco products, and increased levels of usage of those products, are well established. Such advertising and promotion could easily drive a similar expansion in psychoactive drug usage.

Therefore, the default position of any licensing regime should be a complete ban on all advertising, promotion or marketing of all drugs, with any exceptions made only on a cautious case by case basis by the relevant authorities. This ban should include any alcohol and tobacco marketing activities. A default ban should also exist on political donations from any commercial operators in the drugs market.

The distinct nature of drug risks relative to most other commodities, and the particular need to protect vulnerable groups from exposure to these risks, (see discussion of *Regulated Market Model*, page 27) justifies this stringent restriction of standard commercial freedoms. These controls should extend to point of sale advertising, and the external appearance and signage for outlets.

Such controls should be as strict as possible, within the context of local legal regimes. For example, in the US, a free speech argument can be made against such a ban. However, even though the Supreme Court has extended a degree of *'free speech'* protection to commercial speech, such speech is still subject to various controls and limitations.

3.4.2 Location/density of outlets

Location and density of bars and off-licences has been shown to have an impact on patterns of alcohol use and misuse.[18] Controlling the location and density of legal drug outlets—whether licensed sales sites or venues combining sale and consumption—could help limit and control usage in potential problem areas. It should be noted that this would aim to help prevent over-availability, rather than reduce it to zero (which might, in any case, create illicit sales opportunities). Similarly, restrictions could be placed around specific sites of public concern. These could include schools or other places where young people gather.

3.4.3 Shared responsibility between supplier and consumer

As a way to ensure responsible vendor conduct, licensing agreements

---

[18] *'Current Research on Alcohol Policy and State Alcohol and Other Drug (AOD) Systems'*, State Issue Brief by National Association of State Alcohol and Drug Abuse Directors (NASADAD), 2006, page 5.

could include elements of shared responsibility between provider and consumer. The provider would be held partially responsible/liable for consumer behaviour. This would encourage vendors—and, in particular, consumption venue proprietors—to monitor the environment where the drug is used, and restrict sales based on the behaviour of the consumers (see also: *3.5.2 Degree of intoxication of purchaser*, page 55).

Proprietors could be held part-responsible for socially destructive incidents (such as automobile accidents). This responsibility would extend for a specified period of time after the drug is consumed. Sanctions could include fines or licence revocations. Of course, the consumer would not be absolved of responsibility for such incidents; a clearly defined balance based on joint liability would be established. This is admittedly a potentially tricky area of regulation to establish and police, but precedents relating to alcohol vending do exist in Canada, the US and elsewhere.

3.4.4 Volume sales/rationing controls

Sales to individual purchasers could be restricted to levels deemed appropriate for personal consumption. This would:

* Prevent or minimise unlicensed selling on or gifting of the product to a third party
* Reduce opportunities for excessive use

Of course, problems would arise when an individual wants to procure a larger amount. This creates an incentive for any restrictions to be circumvented, through, for example, purchases from multiple sources, or product stockpiling. It must be acknowledged that any rationing system, whilst being able to limit or contain some behaviours in some circumstances (larger scale bulk-buying for example), will be imperfect and—with enough will and determination—can be circumvented.

Secondary tiers of regulation could be put in place if such circumvention becomes especially problematic. The most obvious current example of a volume control/rationing system is that used to manage existing prescribed drugs. This includes systems designed to help maintain dependent users, some of which require frequent repeat prescriptions or daily pick ups. These latter examples are extremely strict management methods, which are hard to justify in cases other than the highest risk drugs/preparations, or in support of maintenance prescribing.

More generally, purchase tracking linked to a centralised database, in conjunction with an ID based licensed purchaser scheme (see below) could to some degree prevent multiple purchasing and stockpiling. However, such a system would be potentially bureaucratic and expensive, and could also raise privacy concerns; many would view it as being overly intrusive.

Comparable systems do, however, already exist for certain controlled prescribed drugs, such as the *Pharmanet* system in British Colombia, Canada, under which all prescriptions for certain drugs are centrally tracked and all physicians and pharmacists have access to the network database.[19]

Combining price controls with purchase tracking could create a system of progressive price increases to act as a progressive financial disincentive to bulk buying (rather than absolute ban)—the price rising as more is purchased.

Familiar volume rationing systems also exist for duty free purchase of alcohol and tobacco, although they are specifically aimed at preventing commercial sales to third parties, rather than misuse *per se*. In the Netherlands, an upper limit of five grams of cannabis for individual purchasers is a licensing condition for the country's cannabis coffee shops.

19   For more details about Pharmanet and how it operates see: www.health.gov.bc.ca/
     pharme/pharmanet/netindex.

3.4.5 **Time delay between order and pick up**

An order/pick up time delay would encourage forward planning of any drug taking, and thereby more responsible use and moderation. This would also help curtail binge use, by preventing immediate access to further drug supplies once existing supplies had run out. In some countries access to casinos is controlled in this way; membership is required for entry, but it is only activated the day after application.

3.5 **Purchaser and end user controls**

3.5.1 **Age of purchaser controls**

Restricting or preventing access to drugs by non-adults is a key element of any existing or future regulatory models. Any rights of access to psychoactive drugs and freedom of choice over drug taking decisions should only be granted to consenting adults.

> Any rights of access to psychoactive drugs and freedom of choice over drug taking decision should only be granted to consenting adults

This is partly because of the more general concerns regarding child *vs.* adult rights and responsibilities. More importantly, however, the specific short and long term health risks associated with drug use are significantly higher for children; and, of course, the younger they are, the greater the risks.

This combination of legal principle and public health management legitimises a strict age control policy. In practical terms, it should also be noted that stringent restrictions on young people's access to drugs—whilst inevitably imperfect—are more feasible and easier to police than population wide prohibitions. Generally speaking, children are subject to a range of social and state controls that adults are not. More specifically, drug restrictions for minors command near universal adult support.

Combined with this is the fact that—while markets created by any prohibition will always attract criminal interest—the non-adult market for drugs is a small fraction of the total adult market. Thus, enforcement resources could be brought to bear on it with far more efficiency, and correspondingly greater chances of success.

It is also worth pointing out that one ironic and unintended side effect of prohibition can often be to make illegal drug markets, that have no age thresholds, easier for young people to access than legally regulated markets for (say) alcohol or tobacco.

Of course, there is an important debate around what age constitutes adulthood and/or an acceptable age/access threshold. Different countries have adopted different thresholds for tobacco and alcohol, generally ranging from 14 to 21 for purchase or access to licensed premises. Where this threshold should lie for a given drug product will depend on a range of pragmatic choices. These should be informed by objective risk assessments, evaluated by individual states or local licensing authorities, and balanced in accordance with their own priorities. As with all areas of regulatory policy there needs to be some flexibility allowed in response to changing circumstances or emerging evidence.

In the UK for example, the age of access for tobacco purchase has recently been raised from 16 to 18, whilst in the US there is a growing debate over whether the alcohol age threshold of 21 is too high. The Amethyst Initiative[20] for example (supported by 135 chancellors and presidents of US universities and colleges) argues that the 21 limit has created *'a culture of dangerous, clandestine "binge-drinking"—often conducted off-campus'* and that *'by choosing to use fake IDs, students make ethical compromises that erode respect for the law.'* Even within a legal regulatory framework, inappropriate prohibitions evidently have the potential to create unintended consequences. They can undermine, rather than augment, social controls and responsible norms around drugs and drug use.

It is clear that age limits need to be realistic and, crucially, properly enforced for them to be effective. In the UK for example—where *'binge-drinking'* amongst young people has been a growing problem—there has been a widespread lack of age restriction enforcement, Alcohol Concern reporting that: *'10–15% of licensed premises are found to persistently sell alcohol to the under-aged yet only 0.5% licensed premises are called up for review'.*[21] Secondary supply of legitimately obtained drugs to non-adults will also require appropriate enforcement and sanction, perhaps with a graded severity depending on distance in age from the legal threshold.

Legal age controls can, of course, only ever be part of the solution to reducing drug-related harms amongst young people. Effective regulation and access controls must be supported by concerted prevention efforts. These should include evidence based, targeted drug education that balances the need to encourage healthy lifestyles (including abstinence) while not ignoring the need for risk reduction and, perhaps more importantly, investment in social capital. Young people—particularly those most at risk in marginal/vulnerable populations—should be provided with meaningful alternatives to drug use. The SMART programme in the US, which works on public housing estates, has found that providing youth clubs has a real impact on reducing drug use, dealing and overall criminal activity in both young people and adults.[22] It is also worthy of note that The Netherlands and Sweden regularly top the United Nations Children's Fund (UNICEF) child well-being[23] table and have relatively low levels of drug misuse, whilst the US and UK invariably sit at or near the bottom and have relatively high levels of misuse and a lower age of misusers.

Whilst steps to restrict access and reduce drug use amongst young people are important, it is also essential to recognise that some young

21 *'Unequal Partners: A report into the limitations of the alcohol regulatory regime'*, Alcohol Concern, 2008, page 19.

22 Steven P. Schinke, *et al.*, *'The Effects of Boys & Girls Clubs on Alcohol and Other Drug Use and Related Problems in Public Housing. Final Research Report'*, Education Resource Information Center, 1991.

23 *'Child poverty in perspective: An overview of child well-being in rich countries, Innocenti Report Card 7'*, UNICEF, 2007, page 4.

people will still access and take drugs. It is vital that they should be able to access appropriate treatment and harm reduction programmes without fear.

3.5.2 Degree of intoxication of purchaser

This form of control combines shared responsibility between user and vendor with an understanding that drug taking choices should be based on informed consent and responsible decision making, both of which can be compromised by intoxication.

A number of countries have established a precedent for this kind of control by making it illegal to sell alcohol to people who are drunk,[24] both through off and on-sales. However, such regulation is problematic, as it tends to be poorly or unevenly exercised and rarely enforced.[25] Some of these problems are explored below, along with potential solutions that could increase the effectiveness of this kind of regulatory regime.

ISSUES/PROBLEMS

What is the threshold level of intoxication beyond which vending and purchasing is restricted? What criteria should be used to establish it? How do you determine if someone has passed it? Without the impractical deployment of breathalyser or similar technology, or more detailed impairment testing, there is a large degree of subjectivity involved in such judgments (particularly difficult if in bar/club environments that are crowded, noisy, busy, or poorly lit).

RESPONSES/SOLUTIONS

> To avoid the more subjective marginal cases, only fairly extreme intoxication would qualify for restriction of sales where a clear-cut series of guideline criteria would have to be met. It would be necessary for these criteria to be well understood by both vendors and patrons (see below). Investment would need to be made in public education so patrons know what to expect.

> Provision of methadone in Canada, for example, is contingent on the patient

---

24 For example the UK Licensing Act 2003, Part 7/141.

25 A parliamentary answer from the UK Home Office (March 19, 2008) reveals that annual prosecutions for serving a drunken patron remain at zero or in single figures in most areas of the UK.

appearing lucid and not overly sedated. Pharmacists are liable if they give a dosage which results in harm or death.

ISSUES/PROBLEMS

Third party purchasing on behalf of an intoxicated individual.

RESPONSES/SOLUTIONS

> In theory it could be made a civil offence to knowingly buy a drug for someone who has been denied service. However, this would add a further complication to enforcement efforts and may not be realistic in practice.

> It has to be acknowledged that the system is imperfect; encouraging licensee and premises staff vigilance and responsibility is the best approach.

ISSUES/PROBLEMS

When denied service, irate, aggrieved and highly intoxicated customers present potential security, public order and safety problems for vending staff and others. (This is a problem more often encountered with alcohol than any other drug intoxication.)

RESPONSES/SOLUTIONS

> Health and safety precautions for staff could include security staff on premises, or physical barriers between vendor and purchaser.

> Clear, easy to refer to on-site information about rules of service.

> Investment in better public understanding of the law.

> Staff training in dealing with difficult customers.

ISSUES/PROBLEMS

Lack of staff skills. Bar staff are frequently low paid, working on a temporary, transitory or informal basis, unlicensed, and lack any training in this regard.

RESPONSES/SOLUTIONS

> A low threshold licensing scheme for bar staff could be explored, which would include a requirement for relevant basic training.

> Licensees could be made liable for bar staff misdemeanours, thus ensuring minimum levels of staff training.

> In Canada (and in Utah, USA), bar owners and home servers can be held liable if the

customer or guest drinks and then has a car accident. Penalties are fines for the owner (and possibly the server); licence to serve alcohol can also be removed.

ISSUES/PROBLEMS

The profit motivation of commercial vendors, and the need to maximise sales in a highly competitive market place (many franchise pub managers work towards very tight volume sales targets) will naturally create a tendency *against* restricting sales.

Whilst it may not be the norm, many people go to the bars specifically to get intoxicated, and the industry profits from and to some extent encourages precisely the sort of excessive intoxication that such theoretically industry enforced regulations are attempting to restrict.

RESPONSES/SOLUTIONS

> This is essentially a carrot and stick issue: on the one hand a culture should be encouraged whereby vendors understand that it's in their long term interests to follow the regulations, and on the other public resources should be put into educating vendors and customers about it and then enforcing it more effectively.

> Effective implementation of such a regulation would hopefully over time help establish social norms defining socially acceptable levels of public intoxication.

A similar principle operates in pharmacies. Pharmacists are required to restrict or refuse sales of certain prescription and over the counter products if they suspect intoxication, or potential non-medical product use or misuse. However, pharmacies are highly regulated environments, and pharmacists are highly trained, and respected, professionals. This means that pharmacy staff face few of the problems associated with bars or clubs, where the drug in question is unambiguously being consumed on the premises for the purpose of recreational intoxication.

Given this, it seems reasonable to conclude that premises licensed for sales only, rather than for sale and on site consumption, are better positioned to implement such restrictions, although they are also less likely to need them. However, there may still be a need for them to consider some of the issues raised above. For example, in Canada methadone prescriptions can order *'witnessed ingestion'* of methadone. In this case, patients have to drink the *'juice'* in front of the pharmacist, who has to note that they were not intoxicated.

Particular issues arise for pharmacists supplying dependent users with prescriptions for either substitute or drug of choice maintenance. A considerable body of experience and well established guidelines for handling the various scenarios and problems associated with this kind of transaction already exists.

Licensed premises for the consumption of cannabis are a good example of where such regulations might come into force under future, less restrictive drug availability regimes. Experience in Holland and elsewhere suggests that cannabis use is on the whole, self regulating, and unlikely to cause major over-intoxication problems. In this case, the main intoxication related restriction of sales would be for people who are either drunk, or using other drugs. If they then seek to purchase or consume cannabis, guidelines comparable to those that exist for alcohol vending premises could come into force.

3.5.3 Licences for purchasers/users

A system for licensing purchasers/users presents the opportunity to introducing a range of different controls.

Obtaining a licence to purchase or possess a given drug could, for example, be like obtaining a driving licence, or pyrotechnics licence to buy and use certain fireworks. It could be dependent on passing a test, which would establish that the licensee knows and understands the risks inherent in drug use, and is thus well placed to make responsible consumption choices.

This is a potentially flexible system:

* Drug access licences could to some degree control time, place and associations for new users, just as newly licensed drivers are sometimes restricted as to where and when they drive, and who they are permitted to drive with.

* Like a driving licence, violations of licence conditions could be associated with hierarchy of penalties. These would depend on the seriousness of violation, and could lead to licence and access suspension once a points threshold had been passed. Such offences might include consuming in public, passing/ selling drugs to non licensed individuals, or driving under the influence. Such penalties would need to be balanced with any concurrent civil or criminal sanctions.

* The variable licensing system could also function as a graduated program, specifying different levels of access to various products based on levels of additional training, or periods of good conduct or maintenance of a clean licence.

* Purchaser licences could be linked to an ID system, to prove that the purchaser is the licensee. Such ID might feature the same sorts of electronic identification systems (embedded biometric data, etc.) as other established ID card/driving licence models, or licences could be embedded or electronically linked to an existing ID system.

From a public health and harm reduction perspective, licence applicant training programmes would offer an invaluable opportunity to augment drug and health education for a key target population. Information could be directed to drug users about risk, dependency, treatment services and other health issues. Care would need to be taken to present an educational element without being over-burdensome, condescending or preachy.

The programs could, using established prevention education methods, harm reduction principles and motivational techniques, furnish graduates with key drug related knowledge and skills. These would empower them to make independent drug use choices, reduce associated harms, cultivate social norms supporting responsible, moderate use, promote abstinence as the zero risk option, and provide an understanding of the rights and responsibilities of drug users.

As touched on in *3.4.4 Volume sales/rationing controls* (page 50), licensed users could have their purchase volume and frequency tracked. This data could be used to highlight potential problematic usage patterns. If a problem comes up, the dispensing pharmacist could instigate a *'health intervention'*. He or she could register their concerns with the user, and offer relevant assistance. The tracking may be a deterrent to use in itself. It could also be tied to other deterrent effects; for example, price increases could be triggered once the user has passed a certain purchase volume threshold. Users could also put a stop purchase order on their licence themselves, should they wish to avoid temptation. Such an order would deactivate their access to a given drug for a given period.

3.5.4 **Proof of residency with purchase**

Some societies have developed *'culturally specific social controlling mechanisms'* that—over time—have allowed their members to form relatively healthy, unproblematic relationships with certain drugs. There is a possibility that *'drug tourists'*, who have not been integrated into this culture, may not adhere to the local restraining social practices, potentially leading to problematic or risky behaviours.

To help avoid such behaviour, purchasers could be restricted to residents of a country, state/province, city or even a particular neighbourhood. This would however require a residency-linked ID system, which is itself not without problems.

3.5.5 Required membership in club or group prior to purchase

Drug users could join membership clubs or groups[26]. These would work in a similar way to existing professional regulatory bodies. They would provide access to specific drugs, along with clearly defined good practice guidelines for their members. If the user acts outside of the norms or rules of the group, membership can be refused or revoked. The norms are communicated through education, and enforced through a variety of formal and social peer processes.

Alternatively, licensed venues could use a membership model based on those used to restrict access to casinos or late night drinking venues in some countries.[27] Such a model could potentially be applied to venues licensed for the sale and consumption of certain drugs, as a core licence condition. The membership based venue or club model allows for various other controls to be put in place, as appropriate. These can include:

* Time delay between application for membership and first use of venue (in the UK casino model a 48 hour delay was used), or time delay between order and delivery
* Conditions of membership including training or interview
* Consumption on premises only—no sales of *'take outs'*
* Venue licensing conditions *(see above)*

3.5.6 Controls over permitted locations for use

One of the major, if unspoken, anxieties about drug reform is that drug use would be far more visible and socially intrusive. In reality, the new regulatory regimes would make it possible for drug use to be far less visible than at present.

Alcohol and tobacco licensing regimes have established clear precedents

---

26 D. Gieringer, *'Drug User's Clubs: A Modest Proposal'*, unpublished conference discussion paper, (US) Drug Policy Foundation conference, November 1994.

27 As used, for example, in the UK until the Gambling Act 2005 came into force.

Controlled drinking area in the UK

'No injecting' sign in Amsterdam, Netherlands

for defining and controlling permitted substance use locations. A range of flexible controls exist for both, including:

* Licensed premises for consumption of alcohol.

* Designated outdoor smoking areas, gardens, or smoking booths (following the widespread adoption of indoor public space smoking restrictions).

* Zoning laws restricting alcohol use and smoking in specified public and private spaces.

The functions of these restrictions differ. Smoking restrictions are usually justified on the basis of the environmental/secondary health impacts of smoke;[28] public alcohol consumption is more often restricted for public order reasons, and to lesser extent, litter issues. These restrictions are sometimes centrally, sometimes regionally, defined and driven. They are enforced to different degrees, usually through the deployment of fines.

Because they enjoy broad popular support, these restrictions are generally well observed. Experience suggests that when effectively exercised such regulation can foster new social norms, ensuring that less onerous enforcement is needed as time passes.

It is both reasonable and practical to propose that—in the future—similar restrictions would exist for other drugs. For example, public

28 Although most public health benefits probably accrue from reduced levels of use.

smoking bans could naturally extend to cover the smoking of any drug, most obviously cannabis. Restrictions on public intoxication and public disorder that already exist, and that are regularly applied to drunkenness, could be extended to include any form of intoxication. In fact, to some extent they already have been.

Drugs that are in oral pill form, and to a lesser extent powder drugs that are taken orally or snorted, generally present less of a problem in terms of public consumption. The act of consumption itself is brief; it is not part of the drug using experience or ritual in the same way that drinking, smoking, or injecting is.

The use of injecting paraphernalia, whilst only representing a tiny fraction of total drug use, creates a disproportionately large regulatory challenge. Chaotic injecting drug users require particular attention. They are simultaneously most likely to cause hazardous drug litter problems, and least likely take notice of their civic responsibilities.

Given this, it would seem reasonable to ban public injecting. However, experience demonstrates that such bans are only likely to succeed if broader social and harm reduction responses are simultaneously put in place. These include:

*   Accessible needle exchange
*   Provision of safer supervised injecting facilities
*   Housing assistance to deal with homelessness

'No cannabis smoking' sign in Amsterdam. A fifty Euro fine is specified

'No Smoking' sign, UK

* Outreach programs
* Low threshold treatment and service provision
* Access to social and welfare support

Without such policies in place the likelihood is that public injecting will continue, even if geographically displaced. Enforcing anti-injection laws will simply add to the burden of criminality for chaotic users, who frequently are unable to even pay the fines that such laws demand. This will have the effect of pushing them into more dirty and risky marginal environments, without acting as any significant deterrent.

Further reading

* *'A Public Health Approach to Drug Control'*,
  British Colombia Health Officers Council, 2005
* *'Effective Drug Control: Toward A New Legal Framework'*,
  The King County Bar Association, 2005
* *'Thinking Seriously About Alternatives to Drug Prohibition'*,
  E. Nadelmann, Daedalus, 1992; 121: pages 87–132

Making a
regulated
system
happen

4.1   A cautious, phased introduction

Governments and other authorities have significant experience in
regulating potentially harmful recreational products and activities,
including a broad range of psychoactive drugs. However, developing
and implementing new legal regulatory models for currently illegal
drugs is essentially working from a blank slate. This presents clear
opportunities to learn from past policy successes and failures, but also
risks unintended or unanticipated negative consequences.

For certain elements of the reform agenda—for example incorporation
of human rights principles and law into international drug control—a
rapid change is warranted. For other elements of the reform process,
such as the development of legal supply models and availability controls,
the responsible approach is to phase in change over a period of months
or years. This change should take place along various policy increments,

so that policy and regulatory models can be developed whilst outcomes on key indicators are carefully monitored and evaluated.

This approach should be, by default, based on a precautionary principle, particularly where evidence from existing policy is thin, or specific high-risks are identified. New models will thus initially err towards stricter, more intrusive regulation, with lower restriction levels only subsequently coming into play. A precautionary and incremental approach allows for key concerns, such as availability to youth, increase in high risk behaviours or other specific public health concerns, to be closely monitored. If problems do arise, policy can take a step back, be refined and adjusted, and alternative or additional regulatory tools can be deployed.

Additionally, such an approach has democratic benefits, in that it allows for greater civil society involvement in policy development. It also goes some way to removing the fear that all drugs would somehow just become available *'overnight'*. By demonstrating that policy is being developed in a responsible and cautious fashion, based on evidence of effectiveness and sensitive to legitimate fears and concerns, it offers the opportunity to win a greater level of public and political support for a programme of reform. Such a cautious, measured approach will also help placate critics, who fear that moves towards regulation are a *'gamble'*, un-evidenced or in some way *'reckless'*.

A useful precedent for this is provided by some of the more contentious harm reduction policy developments of the past two decades, such as needle exchanges, supervised injecting venues, or opiate prescribing. Due to the highly charged political environment around drugs issues, such interventions have been subject to unprecedented regulation and scrutiny. Particular attention has been given to their effectiveness in reducing health harms, and to high profile concerns that they can somehow encourage use. Responses to such scrutiny have demonstrated how effective policy interventions can be developed, public concerns can be dealt with sensitively, sensationalist media coverage responded to intelligently, and political opposition ameliorated.

The increments along which phased change can be implemented are essentially in line with the range of regulatory tools described in chapters two and three. There is the potential to move from greater to lesser levels of regulation, controlling the levels of availability either through deployment of the different regulatory controls over suppliers, purchasers and products, or through their deployment at varying intensities. Where possible the longer term aim would be to encourage and move from legal/administrative controls towards social controls.

Different countries will necessarily take different approaches, and see their policy and legal infrastructure develop along different routes. There will, for example, be very different challenges faced by primarily producer, transit or consumer countries, states with different levels of economic resources, political stability and public health and enforcement infrastructure, and states that are geographically isolated, compared to those with large borders with highly populated regions.

Cannabis is likely to be the first drug to have regulatory models more seriously explored. This is because:

*   It is by far the most widely used illegal drug.
*   Established and effective models already exist for regulating its production and supply (see: pages 206 and 110).
*   Public opinion is generally both supportive of reform (approaching or having reached majority support in many countries) and growing.[29]

At the other end of the spectrum, around problematic dependent use of opiates and stimulants, we are likely to see medicalised maintenance

---

29 R. Newcombe, *'Attitudes to drug policy and drug laws; a review of the international evidence'*, Transform Drug Policy Foundation, 2004.

prescription models developed and expanded. These models will be based on already established, functional and effective interventions in numerous countries. These two emerging trends are already defining an ongoing pragmatic reform process —addressing the areas of most pressing practical necessity where prohibition's effects are the most egregious, in population terms (cannabis) and overall harm creation (chaotic use/dependence).

Within broad groupings of similar types of drugs—stimulants, depressants or hallucinogens (see: *chapter 5*)—we might reasonably expect regulated legal availability pilots to begin by focussing on the drugs least likely to be associated with personal or social harms and costs (see: *4.2 Assessing drug harms*, page 70). Similarly, less potent preparations of drugs, for use through lower risk methods of administration, could be made available in the first instance. So, for example, psilocybin (*'magic'*) mushrooms might be made initially available, rather than LSD, opium rather than pharmaceutical opiates, and lower potency orally consumed stimulants rather than cocaine powder or methamphetamine.

4.2 Assessing and ranking drug harms

The concept of quantifying and ranking drug harms has two primary functions. First, such rankings should inform policy makers, so that they can develop effective, targeted and proportionate policy responses to a range of different drug harms, which can thereby be managed and minimised. This is an essential element of developing effective regulatory frameworks and inevitably requires a degree of population based generalisation. The second is to facilitate the education of individuals about drug risks and harms, so enabling them to make informed and responsible decisions about their health and wellbeing. This requires information that is more nuanced and person-specific in nature.

Getting to grips with these questions requires that two important distinctions are made. First of all, primary health harms to individual users should be distinguished from the secondary social harms to third parties that follow from that use. Second, harms related to drug use *per se* (both primary and secondary) should be distinguished from harms created or exacerbated by policy environments. The prevailing analysis that informs most current policy makes the first distinction (between health and social harms) reasonably well, but largely fails to make the second distinction (between drug harms and policy harms). It confuses and conflates the two, often misattributing prohibition or illicit market harms to drugs, or by default drug users, and feeding the self-justifying feedback loop that has helped immunise prohibition from scrutiny.[30]

Some efforts to untangle drug use harms from drug policy harms have been made, although this is an area that warrants more detailed consideration and analysis. Transform's 2004 publication *'After the War on Drugs: Options for Control'*[31] describes six key harms created by prohibition (each then broken down into sub-categories): *'creation of crime'*; *'a crisis in the criminal justice system and prisons'*; *'billions in wasted expenditure and lost tax revenue'*; *'undermining public health and maximising [health] harms'*; *'destabilising producer countries'* and *'undermining human rights'*. Correspondingly, the Transform report then makes a distinction between the aims of the drug policy reform movement—to reduce or eliminate the harms specifically created or exacerbated by prohibition and illicit markets—and the more conventional aims of an effective drug policy—to reduce or eliminate the range of direct and indirect harms associated with drug use and misuse.

A more comprehensive *'taxonomy of drug-related harms'* has been constructed by MacCoun and Reuter[32] who break down forty six identified drug-related harms into four general categories: *'health'*, *'social and economic functioning'*, *'safety and public order'*, and *'criminal justice'*.

30 For a more detailed discussion of disaggregating drugs use and drug policy harms see: *'A Comparison of the Cost-effectiveness of the Prohibition and Regulation of Drugs'*, Transform Drug Policy Foundation, 2009.

31 *'After the War on Drugs: Options for Control'*, Transform Drug Policy Foundation, 2004, page 9.

32 R. MacCoun, P. Reuter, *'Drug War Heresies'*, Cambridge University Press, 2001, page 106.

The nature of drug preparation, how the drug is administered, and the physical and social/peer environment in which consumption takes place are also crucially important linked variables in determining risk

In tabular form they then identify six population group headings ('*users*', '*dealers*', '*intimates*', '*employers*', '*neighbourhood*' and '*society*') and note which of these '*bears the harm/risk*' for each of the harms listed. Crucially, in a separate column they also identify what they term the '*primary source of harm*' for each of the populations, from three options: '*use*', '*illegal status*' and '*enforcement*' (illegal status and enforcement being identified for thirty six of the list).

The task of assessing and ranking drug harms is clearly complicated by the large number of variables involved, the permutations of which make attempting to describe and categorise drug harms and risks a complex challenge. Policy the world over is currently based on grouping illegal drugs into between three and five harm rankings (for example the A-B-C classification system in the UK, the I-IV scheduling system in the US). Whilst these systems have some functionality, they are frequently both inconsistent and oversimplified. On a practical level, they are built on generalisations, they (confusingly) fail to include legal drugs, and both conflate and fail to fully acknowledge multiple harms; this has substantially reduced their utility, both as policy making tools, and as aids to individual users seeking to make informed decisions about personal drug use.

Before discussing these issues and their policy implications in more detail it is worth trying to deconstruct the main vectors of harm associated with drug use specifically (as distinct from harms related to drug policy) that policy makers must consider.

4.2.1 **Breakdown of drug health risks/harms**

The personal health risks/harms associated with a particular drug are most usefully divided into toxicity and '*addictiveness*'—that is, a drug's propensity to cause dependence. The level of risk associated with a given drug's toxicity and propensity to cause dependence is then moderated by a series of behavioural variables, and by the predispositions of the individual user. These can be described on an individual or on a population/sub-population basis.

i   **Toxicity**

A distinction needs to be made between short term acute toxicity (for example, death following respiratory arrest from a heroin overdose) and long term chronic toxic effects (for example, death from liver cirrhosis after decades of heavy drinking).

A drug's acute toxicity relates to the size of the margin between an active threshold, the dose at which the drugs effect (or desired effect) is achieved by the user, and the dose at which a specified toxic reaction, or overdose, occurs. Such a toxic reaction could involve merely unpleasant temporary side effects, such as vomiting, dizziness, fainting, distress, etc., or a range of more serious acute episodes, tissue damage of some variety, or death.

The comparable terminology for medical drugs is the *'therapeutic index'*, which is the ratio of the therapeutic dose to the toxic dose. With non-medical drugs acute toxicity of a given drug is often measured by assessing the ratio of lethal dose to the usual or active dose. The smaller this gap between active and toxic dosage, the more toxic a drug is deemed to be. Other methods for measuring toxicity, such as sub-lethal toxic effects, also exist; all are clear and relatively simple.

When ranking drugs, however, issues of acute drug toxicity are complicated by a number of behavioural variables, most obviously including mode of drug administration, and poly-drug use. The development of individual tolerances is another complicating factor.

By contrast, long-term chronic drug toxicity is intrinsically more diffi-cult to quantify, especially for new or emerging drugs. It is especially hard to establish individual effect causality in the context of a range of lifestyle variables, and use of multiple drugs. Even when credible esti-mates or measurements can be made of long term effects, the problem arises that rankings of drugs by acute and chronic toxic effects do not necessarily match up.

So, drugs cannot necessarily be usefully grouped together. For example, it is difficult to compare tobacco smoking, which involves low acute risk but high chronic risk, with opiate use, which has high acute risk but lower chronic risks.

ii **Addiction/Dependence**

Historically, the political discourse on drug harms has been dominated by the concept of addiction. The original rankings made in the 1961 UN Single Convention on Drugs, the model for most subsequent domestic ranking systems, were largely predicated on contemporary under-standings of addiction[33] at the time of the treaty's drafting—that is, in the 1940s and 1950s.

Drug addiction, or drug dependence as it is generally now described, is a difficult concept to precisely define, or to achieve consensus on. The WHO and American Psychiatric Association DSM criteria prob-ably come closest to this, but the subject is still the source of endless controversy, not least the fact that addiction is commonly defined as a mental health problem. However, more agreement does exist on the physiological components of drug dependence, described in terms of brain chemistry (neurotransmitters, receptors, etc.). These physiolog-ical components have been well described in the medical literature of the last century (for established drugs at least, if not perhaps so well for more recently emerging ones), and are now well understood.

---

33 The preamble that frames the 1961 convention includes the following: '*Recognizing that addiction to narcotic drugs constitutes a serious evil for the individual and is fraught with social and economic danger to mankind.*'

It is both possible and useful to quantify and thus rank the degree to which a particular drug will tend to be associated with the development of tolerance and specific withdrawal symptoms. An additional physiological aspect of drug action that impacts on dependence is its half life, which measures how long the drug effect lasts. Shorter acting drugs lend themselves to more intensive repeated usage. The qualitative nature of the initial onset of the intoxication experience, or 'rush', and the post-rush experience—the subjective pleasure associated with using the drug—are also important variables. They are, however, harder to objectively quantify, and also dependent to a significant extent on drug preparation, dosage and mode of administration.

However, while the physiological elements of drug action as it relates to dependence can be assessed and potentially ranked, dependency issues are dramatically complicated by the individual user, and the range of psycho-social factors that interface with physiological processes. This interaction produces dependency-related behaviours, which may require the attention of policy makers and service providers. The psycho-social influences upon, or components of dependency relating to, a given drug are far harder to quantify and rank, and far more contentious in the literature. For example, psychological dependence— 'addiction'—is now also associated with sex, shopping, gambling, the internet and so on.[34]

These psycho-social components are, however, arguably no less important in terms of determining behaviours. Some drugs that have relatively moderate or low physiological dependency effects are none the less frequently associated with powerful psychological dependency, cocaine being an obvious example. Whether physiological and psychological dependence should be pooled together in rankings remains a moot point—as does the question of whether 'addiction' remains a useful term, as opposed to dysfunctional, problematic or dependent use.

[34] There is a useful discussion of the issues around how addiction is conceptualised in B. Alexander, 'The Globalisation of Addiction: A Study in Poverty of the Spirit', Oxford University Press, 2008.

iii   **Individual predispositions**

Even if the different vectors of drug harms described above can be meaningfully quantified and ranked, in generalised population terms at least, complications remain. In particular, risk assessment is made more difficult by the wide variation in physiological and psychological makeup of individual drug users. Key variables include general physical and mental health, and age (young and old are more vulnerable). Specific physical and mental health conditions can have a major impact on individual risk, and pharmacogenetic factors can also cause vulnerabilities to certain drug harms in certain individuals.

iv   **Preparation of the drug, method of administration, using behaviours**

For all drugs, there is a clear relationship between risk and dose. This is largely unaccounted for by broadly generalised drug harm categories and rankings. Clearly, a small amount of a Class A or Schedule 1 drug will be less risky than a large dose of a drug from a lower schedule.

The related issue of drug potency is also a risk factor. However, in a regulated market, with standardised products and packaging information, the specific risks of unknown potency (and in particular, of unexpectedly high potency) will largely be removed. The issue of relative potency-related risk has probably been overstated as users, if possessed of the requisite dosage information, will rationally dose control to regulate their own risk exposure—or auto-titrate, to achieve the level of intoxication they are seeking.

The nature of the drug preparation, how the drug is administered, and the physical and social/peer environment in which consumption takes place are also crucially important linked variables in determining risk. This is usefully illustrated with the example of coca based drugs—from chewed coca leaf, through coca drinks, snorted cocaine powder, to smoked crack cocaine (see: page 120). All involve cocaine use, but at widely differing levels of risk.

Summary of risk vector for mode of drug administration[35]

INJECTION

The most risky form of administration, not only because the user is immediately exposed to the totality of the dose consumed, and thus risks overdose, but also because injecting itself involves risk of injury and infection.

SMOKING/INHALATION

Exposes the user to the drug effect only marginally slower than injection but allows a greater degree of control over dose and intoxication—so overdose risk is lower. However, it presents an additional risk of chronic damage to the lungs. It is worth noting that the risk of lung damage can be significantly reduced if the drug can be inhaled in a vaporised form,[36] rather than as smoke from a burning process.

SNORTING (INSUFFLATION)

Powder form drugs can be snorted and absorbed through the nasal mucus membranes over a period of minutes. By contrast to the seconds associated with injection, this is lower intensity and gives some degree of control over dosage. There is a moderate risk of chronic damage to nasal membranes.

ORAL CONSUMPTION

The drug is absorbed over a longer time period (an hour or more) in the gut, which is relatively well equipped to deal with foreign substances.[37] Slower release orally consumed drugs will generally be lower risk than rapid release equivalents, as the level of exposure (blood levels) at any given time is reduced—although length of exposure/intoxication is prolonged. Some drugs, including tobacco and coca leaf are held in the mouth and absorbed through the gums.

35 Other less common modes of administration include transdermal patches (used, for example, in medical administration of nicotine replacement therapy, and slow release methylphenidate), and suppositories; also used, perhaps unsurprisingly, almost exclusively for medical purposes.
36 Prescription drug inhalers are a familiar example of how a drug can be absorbed via the lungs without the risk of lung damage associated with smoke. 'Vaporisers' are also commonly used for cannabis consumption.
37 Including a vomiting defence mechanism.

4.2.2 **Secondary social risks/harms**

Disaggregating drug harms and policy harms

Considerations of secondary risks/harms are, like assessments of drug use health risks/harms, complicated by the influences of the policy environment. The reform position is substantially predicated on the observation that both health and secondary social drug risks/harms are increased in the context of illicitly controlled production and supply, and illicit using environments. Whilst there is a great deal of complexity in teasing out these relative risks/harms, the broader point is simply illustrated with a real world example.

Compare two injecting heroin users; the first is committing high volumes of property crime and street sex work to fund their illicit habit. They are using *'street'* heroin (of unknown strength and purity) with dirty, often shared needles in unsafe environments. Their supplies are purchased from a criminal dealing/trafficking infrastructure that can be traced back to illicit production in Afghanistan. They have HIV, Hepatitis C, and a long—and growing—criminal record.

The second uses legally manufactured and prescribed pharmaceutical heroin of known strength and purity in a supervised clinical setting, with clean injecting paraphernalia. There is no criminality, profiteering or violence involved at any stage of the drug's production supply or use, no blood borne disease transmission risk, a near zero risk of overdose death, and no offending to fund use.

Significantly, with this example no speculative modelling is required; these two individuals coexist in a number of countries, where legal heroin maintenance is available alongside the parallel illicit trade. A similar, albeit less dramatic, comparison could be made for most drugs.

While efforts to disaggregate drug risks/harms from policy risks/harms are of vital importance in taking the policy discourse forward, there are demonstrable social and secondary risks/harms associated with drug use. They flow specifically from the nature of a given drug's effects, and relate to intoxication related behaviours, the propensity for dependency, and harms that can result from dependency related behaviour. The UK Academy of Medical Sciences has identified the following potential social drug risks/harms:[38]

* Deprivation and family adversity resulting from unemployment/ loss of income, loss of working days, family/dependent neglect and risk of abuse.

* Criminality associated with use, including public disorder, problems of having a criminal record, and burden on the criminal justice system (including prisons).

* Burden on the drug treatment and social services.

Risks/harms associated with driving, operating machinery or similar whilst competence is impaired by drug use should be included.

4.2.3 Fine tuning policy responses and communication

Generalising about a given drug product's population harms is sometimes essential; for example, it can help define broad policy priorities. However, it is not always appropriate for fine tuning policy responses for specific sub-populations or individuals.

As they currently stand, drug harm assessments and rankings can help with such generalisations. However, they are less effective when it comes to more nuanced responses. We have tried to point out some of the factors that can support such fine tuning; these are demonstrably not present in existing generalised three or four tiered systems.

Such systems are frequently oversimplified, and both unaware of and unresponsive to sub-cultural population behaviours. They also conflate a number of harm vectors whose rankings are demonstrably different. This leads to policy construction based on an understanding that *'drug A is more risky than drug B'*, even though such judgments are often meaningless when translated into real world behaviour and the experience of individual users.

In terms of public health education, current, former, and potential drug users, as well as non-drug users, need tailored information about drug risks and the potential harms they face as individuals. Such information should be responsive to the very different needs of, for example, a healthy 18 year old wondering about ecstasy, a 26 year old with a history of psychotic illness using cannabis, a 36 year old diabetic concerned about cocaine, or a 66 year old with hypertension considering their alcohol use.

Each and every user needs to be able to understand the risks they person-ally run using a particular drug, at a particular dose, at a particular frequency, administered in a particular way, in a given setting.[39] This is the substantial—but by no means impossible—challenge for educa-tors, be they in schools and colleges, providing websites and leaflets, or designing billboards and TV slots.

They need to find ways of making the complexity that has been alluded to above understandable and accessible to a broad population. In partic-ular, they need to address those who are the most vulnerable to drug related harm, but often the hardest to reach.

The detail of how this challenge is best tackled is beyond the scope of this publication, but from this discussion it is clear that the key variables, or vectors of drug harms, need to be separated, quantified and ranked independently. These include: acute and chronic toxicity, propensity for dependency (both physiological and psychological), issues relating to dosage, potency, frequency of use, preparation of drug and mode of administration, individual risk factors including physical and mental health, age and pharmacogenetics, and behavioural factors including setting of drug use, and poly drug use.

---

39 They also need to have information about danger signs that their drug use, or that of their peers, has become, or is becoming, problematic, and the appropriate course of action, including access to support and treatment services.

4.3   Legislating globally, nationally and locally

The arguments made above imply a need to make a wide range of new drug policy decisions and laws. It is important to understand at what political level such choices and legislation should take place. In principle, they do not significantly differ from similar issues in other arenas of social policy and law dealing with currently legal medical and non-medical drugs. On this basis, we suggest below how new drug legislation and management could be integrated into and managed by a range of different kinds of political bodies, running from the international to the intensely local.

* The UN's various agencies would remain responsible for international human rights and trade issues. They would provide the foundation, ground rules and parameters within which individual states can operate, as well as offering guidance and providing a central hub for international drug research and data collection. The UN role would include oversight and guidance on sovereign state rights, as well as responsibilities to neighbours and the wider international community. An additional expanded role would involve overseeing international non-medical drug trade issues, which would operate in parallel to its existing medical drug production oversight role, alongside the World Trade Organization (WTO) and other relevant trade bodies/agreements.

* Individual states would be able to democratically determine their own drug policies and legal frameworks. Such determination would naturally take place within the international legal parameters, rights and responsibilities established by the UN, and by any other international entities/regional governments to which individual states belong. This would set basic standards of justice and human rights that would have—as a baseline—implications for the use of punitive sanctions against drug users, although they would

neither impose nor preclude issues around legal access/supply, or internal domestic drug trade.

* Local and municipal government could determine the detail of lower tier legal issues around regulation, licensing and enforcement, along with drug service/health provision. This would all sit within the parameters and targets established by the national government, and by implication broader international law. Similar frameworks are already well established in a number of countries with regards to licensing of alcohol sales. In the UK, for example, each licensing authority must review entertainment licenses every three years and consult with the chief of police, fire authority, representatives of the licensees and representatives from local businesses and residents. In the US, alcohol policy is largely managed by the individual states, which control manufacture, distribution and sale within their own borders, whilst the federal government regulates importation and interstate transportation. Similarly, individual states in the US and Australia have very different approaches to enforcement of personal cannabis use—ranging from *de facto* decriminalisation (or civil penalties) to punitive criminal sanctions.[40] The federal/state power dynamic generally sees responsibility for most serious crimes falling to federal government with flexibility over less serious crimes and civil offences falling to state authorities.

4.4 Effective research for effective policy

Over the past five decades, prohibition has been a politically important policy for governments worldwide. Its importance has been driven more by a desire to deal firmly with a perceived *'evil'*, and be seen to be doing so, than by a desire to engage directly with a very challenging and complex set of health and social issues. The need to justify such an

---

40 Federal and international law, however, currently prevents exploration of options for legal regulation of non-medical supply.

approach has shaped the drug research agenda. Directly and indirectly, it has encouraged research to be skewed towards demonstrating drug harms, in order to justify and support punitive responses to the *'drug threat'*. This focus on research that justifies firm, punitive action has led to an avoidance of policy research that meaningfully evaluates and scrutinises the actual outcomes of prohibition.

There is, therefore, a clear need to shift the research agenda away from its historical skew towards medical research of drug toxicity and addiction, and towards meaningful policy research. Of course, it remains very important to fully explore and understand drug related health harms. But such an understanding needs to be complemented by careful evaluation of the policies intended to mitigate such harms. In particular, policy outcomes and policy alternatives should be carefully evaluated and explored.

The responsibility for this has historically fallen largely to the non government sector. Government entry into and support of this area would support both the development of new drug management policies and the modification of existing ones. This would ensure most efficient limitation of drug related harms at a local, national and international level, both in the short and long term.

Two key research programs need to be commenced:

* Critics of the prohibitionist approach can and do argue authoritatively that there is strong evidence of the policy approach's overall failure and counterproductive nature. For political progress to take place, however, this critique and analysis needs to be firmly rooted in a comprehensive ongoing body of international (UN) and state government research—in which all policy outcomes are openly and accurately evaluated on an ongoing basis to agreed standards and using an agreed set of policy indicators/measures. We are still some

way from achieving anything remotely approaching this.[41] The paucity of adequate data and analysis regarding current policy is a significant obstacle to understanding the impacts of that policy, and thus to being able to modify or evolve it to maximise its efficacy.

✽   In parallel to more meaningful evaluation and critical engagement with current policy there needs to be substantial investment in exploration of alternative policy approaches. Such research can utilise established analytical tools of a more speculative nature, such as comparative cost benefit analysis and impact assessments.[42] These can augment ongoing and expanded pilot research on regulated production and supply models. Independent research boards that oversee the research agenda and disseminate findings to relevant stakeholders can operate at state and UN level.

4.5   Broader social, political and economic impacts

Illicit drug production and trade has had a range of profound consequences for the social, political and economic development of key producer and transit countries. The impact for them of any transition towards regulated production within the global market will be correspondingly significant. The development consequences of global prohibition—and impacts of any shifts away from it—need to become more central to the drug reform discourse, which has tended to focus on the domestic concerns of developed world user countries. Such consequences should also feature far more prominently in wider development discourse.

Many countries or regions involved in drug production and transit have weak or chaotic governance and state infrastructure—prominent current examples include Afghanistan, Guinea Bissau, and areas of Colombia. Prohibitions on commodities for which there is high demand

---

41   For more discussion see: M. Trace, M. Roberts, A. Klein, *'Assessing Drug Policy; Principles and Practice'* , Beckley Foundation, 2004.

42   For more discussion see: *'A Comparison of the Cost-effectiveness of the Prohibition and Regulation of Drugs'*, Transform Drug Policy Foundation, 2009.

inevitably create criminal opportunities, pushing production, supply and consumption into an illicit parallel economy. Such illicit activity is flexible and opportunistic, naturally seeking out locations where it can operate with minimum cost and interference—hence the attraction of geographically marginal regions and fragile, failing or failed states. Large-scale illicit activity can feed into a downward development spiral. In such a spiral, existing problems are exacerbated and governance further undermined through endemic corruption and violence, the inevitable features of illicit drug markets entirely controlled by organised criminal profiteers.

Most drug producers do not fit the stereotype of cartel gangsters who sit at the top of the illicit trade pyramid, accruing the majority of the wealth that it generates. The farmers and labourers who make up most of the illicit workforce are frequently living in poor, underdeveloped and insecure environments. Their involvement in the illicit drug trade is in large part because of *'need not greed'*, their *'migration to illegality'*[43] primarily a reflection of poverty and limited options. For example, the UNODC has acknowledged that, in Myanmar, *'opium poppy cultivation is a sign of poverty rather than wealth'*.[44]

> Most drug producers do not fit the stereotype of cartel gangsters who sit at the top of the illicit trade pyramid. The farmers and labourers who make up most of the illicit workforce are frequently living in poor, underdeveloped and insecure environments

This discussion requires that we highlight those harms that are specifically either the result of, or exacerbated by, the illicit nature of the drug trade. Of course, that illicit nature is itself the inevitable and direct consequence of opting for an exclusively prohibitionist approach to drug control.

The 2009 Latin American Commission on Drugs and Democracy[45]

---

43 M. Jelsma, *'Vicious Circle: The Chemical and Biological War on Drugs'*, Transnational Institute, 2001, page 26.

44 *'Life in the Wa Hills: Towards Sustainable Development'*, UNODC Myanmar Country Office, 2006, page 3.

45 *'Drugs and Democracy: Towards a Paradigm Shift'*, Latin American Commission on Drugs & Democracy, 2009, page 25.

has identified five major problems that are caused by prohibition, its enforcement, and the illicit trade that it creates:

* *The development of parallel powers in susceptible areas of national States (poor districts within large cities and their periphery; regions far within the interior; frontier areas; and Amazonian territories);*
* *The criminalization of political conflicts;*
* *The corruption of public life (above all police, justice and penitentiary systems);*
* *The alienation of youth and, especially, poor youth;*
* *The dislocation of farmers (more than two million are internally displaced, thousands more are refugees from drug combat in Colombia) and the stigmatization of traditional cultures (a stigma thrown on coca cultivation, a staple plantation of the Andean cultures in Bolivia and Peru).*

To this list could also be added:

* *'Policy displacement'*[46] whereby the political environment (rather than evidence of effectiveness) skews policy focus and resources dramatically towards counterproductive enforcement and eradication efforts, at the expense of social and economic development. Local public health issues, including problematic drug use and drug related HIV/AIDS, are marginalised.
* Development interventions, where they do occur, are distorted by drug war objectives, which means that they are often inadequate in scale and ineffective in design and implementation.
* Environmental destruction—for example the deforestation of Colombia[47] for illicit coca cultivation (exacerbated by displacement from eradication) and pollution from unregulated coca processing.
* Directly fuelling conflict by providing a source of income for insurgents, terror groups, militias and corrupt governments that supports them as they pursue military objectives.

46 A concept flagged up by the UNODC executive director as one of the *'unintended consequences'* of the drug control system. See: *'Making drug control 'fit for purpose': Building on the UNGASS decade'*, UNODC, 2008.

47 Colombia is one of the most bio-diverse nations on earth.

Of course, high worth natural resources, whether legal or illegal, can also fuel conflict; current examples include oil, diamonds and coltan.[48] But their value remains consistently high, regardless of international legal frameworks. By contrast, drug crops such as opium and coca are essentially low value. They have only become high value commodities as a result of a prohibitionist legal framework, which has encouraged development of a criminal controlled trade. By the time they reach developed world users, such is the alchemy of prohibition, that they have become literally worth more than their weight in gold.

By contrast, the licit production of opium and coca (see: *Appendix 2*, page 193) is associated with few, if any of the problems highlighted above. In this legal context, they essentially function as regular agricultural commodities—much like coffee, tea, or other plant-based pharmaceutical precursors.

Under a legal production regime drug crops would become part of the wider development discourse. Whilst such agricultural activities present a raft of serious and urgent challenges to both local and international communities—for example, coping with the whims of global capitalist markets and the general lack of a fair trade infrastructure— dealing with such issues within a legally regulated market framework means they are not additionally impeded by the negative consequences of prohibition, and the criminal empires it has created.

The potential role of existing illicit producer countries in any post prohibition trade, and the inevitable transitional process, raises a series of questions that require more detailed consideration by key agencies, NGOs and academics.

There is potential for long established legal and quasi-legal coca cultivation in the Andean regions continuing or expanding under a revised

---

48 The ore found in the Congo, that produces Tantalum—a mineral essential to manufacture of mobile phones. See: B. Todd, *'Congo, Coltan, Conflict'*, The Heinz Journal, Vol 3, issue 1, 2006.

regulated framework. Rather like coffee, coca production could be subject to fair trade principles, and for non-pharmaceutical coca products, even some form of protectionism along the lines of the EU's *'Protected Designation of Origin'* (PDO), *'Protected Geographical Indication'* (PGI) or *'Traditional Speciality Guaranteed'* (TSG) systems.[49] Inevitably, however, there would be nothing to stop coca cultivation for future legal markets emerging elsewhere, unless the UN drug conventions were, by agreement, adapted to control such production (as with current opium production), or new international trade agreements established to fulfil a similar role.

For the Andean regions, the transition away from illicit coca production would undoubtedly have many benefits. However, it would also have potentially negative impacts, in terms of reduced GDP and reduced economic opportunities for some already marginalised and struggling populations. These negative consequences cannot be ignored, and also need to be built into any development analysis and planning undertaken by domestic and international agencies.

It would also be imperative to manage the influence of any multinational corporations within this trade; Colombia already has bad experiences with companies such as Coca Cola. In extreme cases, membership of trade unions has lead to persecution, abduction and murder. An expanded or revised role for established state coca-market regulators/monopolies, working more closely with UN drug agencies and international trade bodies, presents a more attractive option.

The future for Afghanistan's opium trade, and to a lesser extent opium production elsewhere in Central and East Asia, is more problematic. Opium is already produced around the world; existing licit production for medical use could relatively easily expand into non-medical production (see: *Appendix 2*, page 193). Poppy cultivation would become less attractive for Afghan farmers, as the price support provided by

49 See the relevant EU detail here: www.ec.europa.eu/agriculture/quality/.

global prohibition progressively eroded. Without internationally administered fair trade, and specifically guaranteed minimum prices, they would be unable to compete with the larger industrialised international production.

It may be that as illicit demand contracts something similar to the well-intentioned but ill-conceived *'Poppies for Medicine'* scheme[50] could play a useful role. Existing illicit production could also progressively migrate into a legal fair trade scheme for export, overseen in a similar fashion to existing medical production (most obviously production in India) by the UN drug agencies.

Any contracting illicit market scenarios would, however, have a very different dynamic to current illicit production. They would certainly operate on a smaller scale and, as with coca in the Andean countries, would have major social and economic implications. Positive impacts from reduced criminal profiteering, conflict and instability would be weighed against the short to medium term reduction in economic opportunity and GDP.

More conventional development interventions will be required for coca and opium producers at the bottom of the illicit production pyramid, who have been adversely affected by the progressive contraction of illicit trade opportunities, and for whom transition into any post-prohibition legal trade was not practically or economically viable. Lessons could be learnt from the extensive experience with Alternative Development (AD), a concept which has failed in its goal of reducing overall illicit drug production, but has—when done well—demonstrated how growers can make the transition into non-drug livelihoods. Key points to consider here include:

❖ AD needs to be well-planned and take account of realities on the ground. In the past, it has often been imposed from above as part of an eradication/enforcement strategy; local participation in project development and ownership of programs is essential.

❖   Too often AD has been seen as separate to poverty reduction strategies and national development programmes, when in fact these are inextricably linked.[51] AD needs to be taken out of drug control strategies, and integrated into wider development policy.

❖   AD must be well-financed and include micro-financing for farmers. It must focus on viable crops and viable markets. It needs to recognise the impact of security, development and human rights as well as education, health, governance, and economic opportunities.

A real concern exists, however, that once the drug control and eradication priorities of current policy diminish, so too will the level of concern for, and development resources directed towards impoverished drug producers.[52] They will simply join the broad ranks of marginalised people so commonly ignored or failed by international development efforts. Some responsibility should fall to the consumer countries as any such transition occurs. Perhaps this responsibility could be discharged through a post-drug war *'Marshall Plan'*. Under such a plan, a proportion of former supply-side enforcement expenditure would be reallocated to devastated former drug-producing regional economies. It would help support alternative livelihoods, and develop good governance and state infrastructure. Funding could come from the *'peace dividend'* that would arrive with the end of the drug war, possibly supported by emerging legitimate drug tax income.

The development field as a whole—including both governments and NGOs—has strikingly failed to engage with the role of prohibition in the creation of development problems. Discussion of alternatives to prohibition has been almost zero. Where there has been engagement it has been largely symptomatic (localised attempts to reduce some illicit market and enforcement related harms; conflict resolution, highlighting

51   J. Buxton, *'Alternative Development in Counter Narcotics Strategy: An Opportunity Lost?'*, (publication pending), 2009.

52   A similar concern has been expressed regarding the priority and resources directed into drug treatment post-prohibition, as the crime reduction agenda becomes increasingly irrelevant.

more excessive/military enforcement responses, etc.). It has consistently failed to address the root causes of the problem.

The basic tenets and legal structures of prohibition itself have hardly been challenged at all. They are invariably seen as being an absolute and unchangeable set of legal/political structures, rather than a particular, reversible policy choice. Some of the blame for this failing must fall at the doors of the drug reform movement and its somewhat myopic domestic preoccupations, but to a large extent the lack of engagement is due simply to fear. Discussing alternatives to prohibition is still seen as taboo in many high level policy arenas, especially for the large majority of development agencies that are state funded or operating under the auspices of the UN.

Any forward movement on this issue must begin with a meaningful effort by key international agencies—NGOs, state governments, and the UN—to count the social and economic development costs of the global commitment to prohibition, the *'unintended consequences of drug control'* so eloquently outlined by the UNODC.[53]

Such evaluations will drive and support dialogue on finding new and more effective ways forward. Such evolution should galvanise a wider development field that has, at last, the opportunity to begin addressing this huge and urgent issue, and to create development opportunities that are more effective and therefore more constructive than those that have gone before.

4.5.1 Broader consequences for organised crime

A frequently expressed concern around moves towards legal drug market regulation focuses on the simple question *'what will all the criminals do once the opportunities afforded them by prohibition are removed?'* Clearly the impacts of moves towards legal regulation of

---

53 A. Costa, *'Making drug control "fit for purpose": Building on the UNGASS decade'*, UNODC, 2008.

drug markets will differ at the various levels of the criminal infra-structure and the environments in which they operate. Since reforms will be phased over a number of years and not happen overnight, criminal drug infrastructures will experience a protracted twilight period of diminishing profit opportunities.

Undoubtedly some criminals will seek out new areas of illegal activity and it is realistic to expect that there may be increases in some areas, such as cyber-crime, extortion or other illicit trades. However, crime is to a large extent a function of opportunity, and it is impossible to imagine that there is enough untapped criminal opportunity to absorb the manpower currently operating an illicit drugs market with a turn-over somewhere in the region of $320 billion a year globally. Even given some diversion into other criminal activity, the big picture will undoubtedly show a significant net fall in overall criminal activity in the longer term. Getting rid of illegal drug markets is about reducing *opportunities* for crime.

This concern is a curious one to posit as an argument against reform because it seems, when considered closely, to be advocating prohibi-tion as a way of maintaining destructive illegal drug empires so that organised criminals do not have to change jobs. By contrast, from a reform perspective, the argument is about removing the largest criminal opportunity on earth, not just from existing criminals but, significantly, from future generations of criminals. Ending prohibition holds the prospect of diverting millions of potential young drug producers, traf-fickers, and dealers from a life of crime.

For many involved in the lower tiers of the developed world illicit drug economy, like the lower tiers of developing world drug production, a contracting illicit trade may have negative consequences, presenting significant short to medium term hardship. Aside from the multiple social harms created by illicit markets, illicit drug markets do create real economic activity and offer employment for many marginalised and socially excluded individuals and populations who have otherwise limited economic choices, particularly in urban centres. Impacts of any more far reaching drug policy reform process on these groups needs to be factored into the social policy discourse as the transition away from prohibition occurs.

"Illicit vice entrepreneurs seem to respond to decriminalizations and shrinkages in illicit markets in any of four ways. Some succeed in making the transition to legal entrepreneurship in the same line of work. Some seek to remain in the business illegally, whether by supplying products and services in competition with the legal market or by employing criminal means to take advantage of the legal markets. For instance, following Prohibition, some bootleggers continued to market their products by forging liquor tax stamps, by strong-arming bartenders into continuing to carry their moonshine and illegally imported liquors, and by muscling their way into the distribution of legal alcohol. Some also fought to retain their markets among those who had developed a taste for corn whiskey before and during Prohibition. The third response of bootleggers and drug dealers is to abandon their pursuits and branch out instead into other criminal activities involving both vice opportunities and other sorts of crime. Indeed, one potential negative consequence of decriminalization is that many committed criminals would adapt to the loss of drug dealing revenues by switching their energies to crimes of theft, thereby negating to some extent the reductions in such crimes that would result from drug addicts no longer needing to raise substantial amounts of money to pay the inflated prices of illicit drugs. The fourth response—one that has been and would be attractive to many past, current, and potential drug dealers—is to forego criminal activities altogether.

"Relatively few criminal pursuits can compare in terms of paying so well, requiring so few skills, remaining fairly accessible to newcomers, and presenting attractive capitalist opportunities to poorly educated and integrated inner-city youth. During Prohibition, tens if not hundreds of thousands of Americans with no particular interest in leading lives of crime were drawn into the business of illegally producing and distributing alcohol; following its repeal, many if not most of them abandoned their criminal pursuits altogether. There is every reason to believe that drug decriminalization would have the same impact on many involved in the drug dealing business who would not have been tempted into criminal pursuits but for the peculiar attractions of that business. The challenge for researchers, of course, is to estimate the relative proportions

of current and potential drug dealers who would respond in any of these four ways. The even broader challenge is to determine the sorts of public policies that would maximize the proportion that forego criminal activities altogether."

E. Nadelmann, *'Thinking Seriously About Alternatives to Drug Prohibition'*,
Daedalus, 1994, 121, pages 87–132

Further reading

Assessing drug harms

* Nutt *et al.*, *'Development of a rational scale to assess the harms of drugs of potential misuse'*, The Lancet, Vol. 369, Issue 9566, pages 1047–1053, 2007

* *'Brain science, addiction and drugs'*, The Academy of Medical Sciences (UK), chapter 5.3: *'Measuring the harm associated with the use of illegal drugs'*, 2008

* Transform submission to the Parliamentary Science and Technology Select Committee inquiry: *'Scientific advice, risk and evidence: how the government handles them — case study on the classification of illegal drugs'*, 2006

* M. Roberts, D. Bewley-Taylor, M. Trace, *'Monitoring drug policy outcomes: The measurement of drug related harm'*, 2006

Effective research

* M. Trace, M. Roberts, A. Klein, *'Assessing drug policy: Principles and practice'*, 2004

Social and economic development

* *'Drugs and Democracy: Towards a Paradigm Shift'*, Latin American Commission on Drugs and Democracy, 2009

* Transnational Institute Drugs and Democracy programme. Visit **www.tni.org**.

Regulated drug markets in practice

5   **Regulated drug markets in practice**

Any discussion of legal drug market regulation must necessarily involve a review of the experiences and lessons learned from different approaches to currently legal drugs, and in particular, alcohol and tobacco. While many mistakes have been made with alcohol and tobacco policy over the past century, more appropriate and effective responses have now been developed, if not universally adopted.

It should be acknowledged that alcohol and tobacco's unique historical, cultural and legal status—and their very distinct effects and patterns of use—do, to some extent, demand a degree of pragmatic realism and flexibility. However, even given this, there can be no good argument made for not developing alcohol and tobacco management policies based on the aims and working principles that drive this book's thinking. The same menu of regulatory tools is available; the same policy outcomes are sought. It is therefore both consistent and necessary to combine moves toward effective legal regulation of currently illegal drugs with calls for improved regulation of currently legal drugs.

In both cases, the unique status of psychoactive drugs as commodities demanding special attention is acknowledged, and the common goal of moving towards optimum regulatory models is shared, even if the movement begins from a different place on the policy continuum and presents a different set of challenges. Likewise, each seeks to achieve the widely shared goals of reducing personal and social harms associated with drug production, supply and use, and the broader promotion of health and wellbeing.

There remains, however, one key difference between managing legal and illegal drugs. The alcohol and tobacco management improvement process has been able to ask, and to some degree answer, questions about which forms of regulation are most effective. These are questions of vital importance; the current legal framework for most other drugs denies us the opportunity to explore them in the context of those drugs, and thus with the full depth and rigour that they both deserve and demand.

A consistent approach to policy across all drugs will help reverse this research gap. It thus holds the prospect of dramatically improving not only policy around currently illegal drugs, but also alcohol and tobacco policy.

5.1 Alcohol

Alcohol policy provides an invaluable body of evidence to support future development of effective legal regulatory models for currently illicit drugs. There is an extensive body of research, publications, and scholarship in the field, by national governments, NGOs, academics, and UN entities including—very prominently—the World Health Organization. Some of this research has been alluded to throughout this book; rather than revisit this well established analysis, this brief discussion will focus more on some of the wider themes that have emerged from it, and their implications for other drugs.

Alcohol is a psychoactive drug that has toxic effects and potential to cause dependence. However, it is important to acknowledge its differences from other drugs. These differences rest on more than just its legal status.

It is unique amongst drugs in that it is a food/beverage. Alcohol itself, being broken down into sugar, has a calorific value. This value is added to by the various beverages, and sometimes foods, with which it is mixed and consumed. Over and above this, many alcoholic beverages have themselves assumed cultural roles and importance only tangentially related to their intoxicating effects. For example, they have been used in cooking, or as components of religious rituals. It is acknowledged that, for example with wine connoisseurs, alcoholic beverages are not consumed exclusively for intoxication.

> For alcohol policy to have an effective future it is clear that potentially very unpopular decisions will have to be made that will involve increasing regulation and heavy restrictions on all aspects of marketing and promotions

Alcohol has a history as old as human civilisation, its use is deeply entrenched in a wide range of social contexts and cultural rituals, throughout a significant majority of the world's societies. With the possible exception of caffeine, alcohol is the most widely used non-medical psychoactive drug. The WHO estimates that there are *'about 2 billion people worldwide consuming alcoholic beverages, and 76.3 million with diagnosed alcohol use disorders'*. The scale of alcohol use and its global cultural penetration help explain why its negative public health impact is only exceeded by tobacco.

If there is any upside to this, it is that a wide spectrum of policy approaches to controlling alcohol have been experimented with, in widely varying social contexts, including unregulated free markets, various formulations of licensed sales, state monopolies, and prohibition. These experiments have taken place across the globe and throughout recent history. From an overview of these experiences, the WHO *'Global Status of Alcohol Policy 2004'* report concludes that:

> *A policy mix which makes use of taxation and control of physical access, supports drink driving countermeasures, and, which invests broadly in treatment of alcohol use disorders and particularly in primary care, advertising restrictions and public awareness campaigns, is, based on all the research evidence, likely to achieve success in reducing the level of alcohol consumption problems (Edwards et al., 1994). Thus, in order to be effective, a comprehensive alcohol policy must not only incorporate measures to educate the public about the dangers of hazardous and harmful use of alcohol, or interventions that focus primarily on treating or punishing those who may be putting at risk their own or others' health and safety, but also must put in place regulatory and other environmental supports that promote the health of the population as a whole.*

This is advice that, with some necessary tweaks and variations, clearly describes the approach to drug policy and regulation being more widely advocated here. Indeed, it is often a revealing experience to read authoritative texts about alcohol control policy, changing the words *'alcohol'* to *'drugs'*, and *'drinking'* to *'drug use'*.[54]

The fundamental conflict between public health policy, and alcohol sale and consumption as a commercially driven activity, is a key issue, coming up repeatedly in alcohol policy literature. This issue raises a series of important concerns for the wider drug policy and law reform agenda. It is rather diplomatically elucidated, for example, in the *'Framework for Alcohol Policy in the WHO European Region'*[55] which notes that:

> *As well as having psychoactive properties, alcoholic beverages are also regarded as commodities. The production and sale of alcoholic beverages, together with the ancillary industries, are important*

---

54 For a paired example see: *'After the War on Drugs: Tools for the Debate'*, Transform Drug Policy Foundation, page 16, 2006.

55 See: www.euro.who.int/document/e88335.pdf.

parts of the economy in many European countries, providing employment for many people, export revenue for drinks companies and substantial tax revenues for governments. These economic and fiscal interests are often an important determinant of policies that can be seen as barriers to public health initiatives. Dissemination of public health research that can counterbalance these economic and fiscal interests is paramount.

Alcohol producers and suppliers see alcohol from a commercial rather than a public health perspective. They do not bear the secondary costs of problematic alcohol use; quite naturally, their primary motivation is to generate the highest possible profits. This is logically achieved by maximising consumption, both in total population and *per capita* terms. Public health issues become a concern only when they threaten to impact on the bottom line, and will invariably be secondary to profit maximisation.

The alcohol industry[56] has historically striven to concede as little market control to regulators as possible. They have achieved this by deploying a now familiar menu of high level lobbying, manufactured outrage and populist posturing (the *'nanny state'* against *'a man's right to have a drink after work'* etc.), dubious science (creating the false impression there is a genuine debate or controversy over issues like the efficacy of price and marketing controls), and token gestures.

In many countries these efforts have been highly effective at distracting from, or delaying, any meaningful regulatory legislation. In addition, they have often successfully kept what regulation has been passed at a voluntary level, meaning that it can largely be ignored or sidelined to the point of being almost completely ineffectual.

The alcohol industry as a whole will never willingly embrace any policies that involve increased or stricter regulation, and that lead to

56 The *'drinks industry'* or *'alcohol industry'* refers to the corporate representatives, and professional bodies, lobbying and PR agencies funded by alcoholic drink manufacturers/suppliers to represent their interests.

a substantial decrease in consumption and profits. Yet this is exactly what is required to address particular issues of binge and problem drinking, and to support the general evolution of a more moderate and responsible drinking culture. It is important to remember that problematic and binge drinking constitute a significant proportion of alcohol industry profits; they are, quite simply, hugely profitable consumer behaviours. Such concerns have prompted adoption of government monopoly control models for sections of alcohol supply in some countries. Examples include the *Systembolaget* system in Sweden,[57] under which the state controls all import and supply, and the provincial government control of alcohol off-licences in some Canadian provinces (Ontario and Quebec). These models have some similarities to the Regulated Market Model proposed for tobacco (see: page 27).

There is a related political problem here, too. As the European WHO report highlights, state governments themselves generate substantial tax revenue from alcohol sales. Furthermore, the alcohol industry is a significant employer of potential voters. These factors combine with the immense lobbying power of alcohol industry bodies, and the public unpopularity of restricting alcohol sales or increasing prices, to create massive political obstacles to effective reforms. This is the case even when knowledge of what works from a public health perspective (that is, encouraging reduced and/or moderate consumption) is clear. In effect, many governments have been complicit in the growing public health crisis associated with alcohol.

For alcohol policy to have an effective future it is clear that potentially very unpopular decisions will have to be made that will involve increasing regulation and heavy restrictions on all aspects of marketing and promotions. How such reforms unfold, combined with historic successes and failures in alcohol control, will continue to provide a rich resource for future, legally regulated markets to learn from.

---

57 In 2007 the EU ruled that the Swedish system violated free trade agreements—raising some difficult questions about the role of state drug controls in a broader international free trade framework.

Further reading

✽   *'Global Status Report: Alcohol Policy'*, World Health Organization, 2004 (public health impacts of alcohol around the world)

✽   *'The Global Alcohol Status Report'*, World Health Organization, 2004 (different policy approaches around the world, and their effectiveness)

✽   *'Working document for developing a draft global strategy to reduce harmful use of alcohol'*, World Health Organization, 2009

✽   *'50 best collection: Alcohol Harm Reduction'*, International Harm Reduction Association, 2008

5.2   **Tobacco**

Tobacco is the most widely consumed psychoactive drug after caffeine and alcohol. It is, however, associated with a disproportionate level of health harms, on a scale that eclipses all other drugs combined. These huge public health impacts are predominantly associated with smoked tobacco; they are related to its high propensity to produce dependency,[58] alongside the fact that it does not intoxicate to a degree that significantly impairs functioning. This combination leads to high frequency dependent patterns of use. Many smokers consume nicotine more than 20 times every day, for prolonged periods—commonly over many years.

Despite the high risks smoking presents (around half of smokers will die prematurely as a result of their use) the low level of intoxication created by nicotine has not historically attracted the moral indignation that fuelled the temperance movement and shaped much punitive prohibitionist thinking on other drugs. As such, tobacco has assumed a unique role in society; a highly visible pattern of dependent drug use associated with a high risk of chronic health harms, yet one that

---

[58] It has a rapid onset, a short half life, is associated with development of tolerance and distinct withdrawal effects and cravings—on top of psychological effects related to habituation into various personal and cultural consumption rituals.

in much of the world, at least until very recently, has become aggressively commercialised and socially acceptable in almost all public environments.

The public health disaster associated with smoked tobacco has, however, ultimately led to the emergence of a range of more pragmatic public health and regulatory responses in a number of countries. Like alcohol, the full gamut of policy responses to tobacco can be observed and learnt from, and there is a substantial body of related scholarship to be drawn upon. There is now a clear consensus around the types of interventions and market regulation that are likely to deliver improved policy outcomes. The World Health Organization sponsored a Framework Convention on Tobacco Control, which provided a good summary of these:

Key policy provisions of the Framework Convention on Tobacco Control (FCTC)[59]

> Increase tobacco taxes

> Protect citizens from exposure to tobacco smoke in workplaces, public transport and indoor public places

> Enact comprehensive bans on tobacco advertising, promotion and sponsorship

> Regulate the packaging and labelling of tobacco products to prevent the use of misleading and deceptive terms such as *'light'* and *'mild'*

> Regulate the packaging and labelling of tobacco products to ensure that appropriate product warnings are communicated to consumers; for example, obligate the placement of rotating health warnings on tobacco packaging that cover at least 30% (but ideally 50% or more) of the principal display areas and can include pictures or pictograms

> Regulate the testing and disclosure of the content and emissions of tobacco products

> Promote public awareness of tobacco control issues by ensuring broad access to effective comprehensive educational and public awareness programmes on the health

59 See the full UN Framework Convention on Tobacco Control here: www.who.int/fctc/en/.

> risks of tobacco and exposure to tobacco smoke

> Promote and implement effective programmes aimed at promoting the cessation of tobacco use

> Combat smuggling, including the placing of final destination markings on packs

> Implement legislation and programmes to prohibit the sale of tobacco products to minors

> Implement policies to support economically viable alternative sources of income for tobacco workers, growers, and individual sellers

Interestingly, this tobacco control convention has 168 signatories, representing a powerful international consensus behind a legal framework dealing specifically with effective non-medical drug market regulation. This level of consensus is notably equivalent to that which exists in support of the three UN drug treaties, which define parallel contrasting systems for the absolute prohibition of almost all other non-medical drug markets (see: *Appendix 1*, page 165).

In stark contrast to those prohibited drugs, in the developed world, tobacco is becoming less, not more, popular; its use has been falling since the 1970s. This is due to a combination of public health education, which raises awareness about previously poorly understood health risks, and increasingly widespread use of market controls like those outlined by the WHO, more recently combined with bans on public indoor consumption. The reining in of the rampant commercial marketing that fuelled the explosion of tobacco use (in particular of cigarettes) in the first half of the last century has been particularly important.

Alarmingly, however, this pattern is far from universal. Tobacco consumption is becoming more popular in large swathes of the developing and newly industrialising world. In these areas, tobacco is being aggressively marketed, often as an aspirational Western lifestyle product—somewhat ironic, given its waning popularity in the West. The commercial forces that have so effectively distorted policy priorities in the past have not lost any of their potential power. They sound a clear cautionary note on the corrupting nature of profit motivations in drug markets.

(See: *Tobacco Regulated Market Model, chapter 2*, page 27)

Tobacco Harm Reduction: Smokeless tobacco

Tobacco harms are substantially related to the inhalation of smoke, rather than the consumption of nicotine *per se*. In common with the regulatory/harm gradient theme explored in the previous chapters, there are public health gains to be had from exploring and developing the market for, and use of, safer, non-smoked nicotine/tobacco products, as alternatives to smoked tobacco.

The increasing use of various nicotine delivery systems, (such as inhalers, gum and patches) as cessation aids is a welcome development, is already widespread, and should be actively supported. Such support could include increased access, as well as a reduction in price (subsidised where necessary) so that those most dependent on nicotine—in particular, those on low income—can afford to access these products.

However, the use of nicotine delivery systems as cessation aids takes place within a medical model that is specifically aimed at achieving abstinence. This is an important and proven part of the public health response to tobacco; it does not, however, cater for those who want to continue consuming nicotine, or will continue regardless of other interventions. Certain non-smoked oral tobacco products (including '*Snus*' and '*Bandits*') offer potential alternative tobacco preparation/consumption methods that are (it is estimated) 90% safer than smoked tobacco.[60]

However, use of such products can only occur if an informed choice is available to the consumer, and will only gain a foothold amongst current smoked-tobacco consumers if they are to some extent promoted as an alternative. In many places they are not widely available; they are, for example, effectively banned from sale across most of the EU.

60 C. Bates *et al.*, '*European Union policy on smokeless tobacco: a statement in favour of evidence based regulation for public health*', Tobacco Control, 2003, Vol. 12, pages 360–367.

Whilst this ban was—like other drug prohibitions—well intentioned, the result is that oral tobacco products that are substantially safer than smoked tobacco are now not available as an alternative to cigarettes.

The oral tobacco product 'Snus' is very popular in Sweden, which has an exemption from the EU sales ban. This is despite a prohibitionist drug policy position that is, in most other respects, the most stringent in Europe. It has been convincingly argued that this high level of oral tobacco use correlates with the fact that the country has the lowest rate of smokers in the developed world. There has been a large drop in the number of smokers in Sweden, in particular within the male population—from 40% in 1976 to 15% in 2002—partially attributed to a roughly corresponding increased use of Snus.[61]

Of course, many healthcare professionals and legislators are understandably unenthusiastic about actively promoting the use of non-smokeable forms of tobacco over nicotine replacement therapies or outright cessation programmes. However, there is plenty of evidence from the Swedish model to suggest that Snus and other similar products can help users give up smoking, as well as providing a safer tobacco alternative.

There are obviously difficult ethical and practical questions regarding how such products can be brought to the market, and then regulated and promoted responsibly; that is, so as to encourage existing smokers to quit or switch from smoked tobacco, while not inducing a fresh tobacco consumption habit in new users. However, these challenges are not insurmountable. The potentially enormous public health gains are such that the relevant agencies should, on pragmatic public health grounds alone, seriously consider the options for appropriate legislative reforms. Research and pilot studies should be commissioned, as appropriate, to explore potential ways forward.

Further reading

* ‘50 Best Collection: Tobacco Harm Reduction’, International Harm Reduction Association, 2008
* R. Cunningham, ‘Smoke and Mirrors: The Canadian Tobacco War’, IDRC, 1996

---

61 J. Foulds *et al.*, *‘Effect of smokeless tobacco (Snus) on smoking and public health in Sweden’*, Tobacco Control, 2003;12, pages 349–359.

Proposed discussion models for currently illegal drugs

First of all, it is very important to reiterate that the proposed models below are just that: proposals intended to trigger further discussion. It should also be acknowledged that the models proposed here reflect the authors' Western background. Other environments, and other user populations, will require different, regionally appropriate ways of thinking. So, we have built a degree of openness and flexibility into these proposals. In particular, we have highlighted potentials for greater or lesser levels of regulation, enforcement and/or deployment of additional controls.

5.3   **Cannabis**

(See also: *3.1.1 Legal cannabis production*, page 35, and *Appendix 2*, page 206).

A large body of literature, research and real world experience can be drawn on to help plot out legal models for cannabis supply and use. In fact, for a drug covered by the UN conventions, cannabis already uniquely spans the drug control spectrum, with examples of almost all regulatory approaches in evidence around the world. These run from extreme prohibition to quasi-legal regulated supply and use.

Of particular relevance is the Netherlands' experience with its unique *'coffee shop'* system, a *de facto* legal licensing of supply and use that has been running since 1976. On one level, the system has problems. A primary issue is the so-called *'back door problem'*; that is, the fact that while both possession and supply from the coffee-shops is tolerated, with the former being effectively legal and the latter licensed, cannabis production itself remains illegal.

This means that coffee shops are forced to source it from an illicit market place. This paradoxical situation is due primarily to the constraints of the UN conventions to which the Netherlands is a signatory.

The fact that the Netherlands' *de facto* legal supply is unique amongst its immediate geographic region has also caused problems of *'drug tourism'* at its borders, with substantial numbers of buyers entering the country solely for procurement. The Netherlands' pragmatic approach has also made them the subject of concerted political attacks and critique from reform opponents on the international stage.

Nonetheless, the licensing models for the coffee shops themselves are well developed. They demonstrably function effectively and without significant problems. Where specific problems have emerged policy has evolved, regulations have been introduced or tightened, and some coffee shops have been closed. Of course, this has not been achieved without some controversy. However, the overall success of the approach has, since its mid-70s introduction, led to growing support from key domestic audiences including the police, policy making and public health bodies, and the general public.

International comparisons are fraught with methodological problems; nonetheless, it is striking that the Netherlands does not have higher levels of use than neighbouring countries, who do not share its tolerant approach and licensed outlets, undermining the simplistic notion that legal availability is the key factor in determining prevalence of use. Certainly, the nightmare scenarios often put forward by opponents of legal regulation have failed to materialise.

More recently, California and other US states have developed medical cannabis supply models. These schemes are often largely indistinguishable from the regulated supply models proposed here for non-medical use. Indeed, somewhat controversially, a proportion of the *'medical'* supply has clearly become a *de facto* non-medical supply infrastructure.[62]

---

62 This is an observation rather than suggested policy path; Transform has written in the past of the need to keep medical and non-medical cannabis issues separate.

Analysis of cannabis health risks have historically become confused with, and distorted by the political debate over the drug's legal status. Viewed objectively, however, the risks associated with cannabis use are well understood and have been exhaustively chronicled. There are particular risks associated with heavy frequent use (especially of stronger/more potent varieties), use by non-adults, use by those with certain mental health problems, and smoking related lung damage—especially when smoked with tobacco.

Acute and chronic toxicity, and propensity for dependence to emerge are both low relative to most other commonly used drugs, including tobacco and alcohol. Most cannabis use is moderate, occasional and not significantly harmful, suggesting that, as elsewhere, the attention of regulators and policy makers needs to focus resources on the minority of users who do, or are likely to experience real problems.

Despite the obvious differences, the nature and extent of cannabis use means that, more than any other currently illicit drug, it lends itself to the lessons learnt from alcohol and tobacco control. As such, the WHO Framework Convention for Tobacco Control (which could almost be adapted for cannabis merely by switching the words, see: page 106), and the WHO guidance on alcohol regulation, provide a sound basis for cannabis regulation models.

Proposed discussion model for regulation of cannabis

BASIC REGULATORY MODELS

> The basic models would involve various forms of licensed sales, for consumption on premises or for take-out—these would be conditional on controls outlined below, and would not preclude a potential pharmacy sales model.

> A regulated market model (see: page 27) might be an appropriate incremental step as legal supply infrastructure and outlets were established. A key task of any regulatory body would be to manage supply so as to prevent the emergence of branded products

and limit all forms of profit driven marketing and promotions.

> Freed from the distorting influence of the non-medical use debate, prescription models supporting medical use of cannabis, or its derivatives, could develop based on evidence. They would assume a much lower profile than is currently the case.

CONTROLS OVER THE PRODUCT

Dosage and preparation:

> Controls could manage the strength/potency of herbal or resin form cannabis, based on relative proportions of active ingredients (that is, ratio of THC [tetrahydrocannabinol] to CBD [cannabidiol]). Maximum and minimum % content could be specified.

> Controls could be put in place to cover potentially toxic contaminants: for example, pesticides, fertilisers, or biological agents such as fungus.[63]

> Different types of cannabis products from different producers could still be identified by name and producer, perhaps with an *'appellation d'origine controllée'* style certification. Generic cannabis products could also be available, subject to the controls outlined above.

> Cannabis prepared for oral consumption (e.g. in cakes or brownies) would need to be sold in appropriately labelled standardised units, based on product weight and active ingredient content/strength per unit. There are particular issues around the difficulty in dosing/self-titrating when cannabis is eaten.

> In much of Europe there is a strong association between the use of tobacco and cannabis which are often smoked together. Legal outlets could be in the forefront of addressing this health concern, helping bring about the cultural and attitudinal changes which would minimise cannabis related tobacco use.

Price controls

> Fixed unit prices or minimum/maximum prices could be specified—with taxation included on a per unit weight or % basis.

> Stronger or more potent preparations could have higher prices/tax rates specified.

> It is likely that prices would be similar to or marginally lower than current illicit

---

63 See for example Netherlands Government guidelines: *'Guidelines for Cultivating Cannabis for Medicinal Purposes: Annex to the Regulation of the Minister of Health, Welfare and Sport of 9 January 2003'*, page 60.

market prices. Prices are relatively low anyway, and the need to de-incentivise illicit production and sale is less pressing than with many other drugs.

Packaging controls

> Tamper proofing - where appropriate.

> Childproof containers (medical pill bottles/canisters).

> Standard labelling—contents (strength/potency), units, health warnings, use by dates etc. Licensed purchaser details as appropriate.

Sales for use on premises would not necessarily have the above requirements.

CONTROLS OVER THE VENDOR/SUPPLY OUTLET

Advertising/promotion

> Cannabis use is embedded in much popular culture. Cannabis products and product iconography are generally non-branded and generic, so a blanket prohibition of anything that might constitute promotion or advertising of cannabis would therefore be impractical. Reasonable controls on exposure to children and young people may be easier to put in place, but would remain difficult to globally define and enforce. However, best practice and evidence from existing controls already widely applied to references to drugs—legal and illegal—in youth media and advertising can be more widely applied.

> Clear lessons can be learnt from experiences with restrictions on promotions and marketing of alcohol and tobacco. Areas where cannabis advertising promotion controls are more realistic include:

> > Advertising for venues for commercial sales could be limited both in content and scope—for example, to specialist publications, or adult only venues. A complete ban on advertising for promotion of venues is not realistic. Dutch coffee shops are not allowed to advertise but do to some extent—the prohibition in practice acts as a moderating influence, rather than a total ban.

> > Restrictions could be placed on appearance and signage of venues/outlets. In the Netherlands, coffee shops are not allowed to make external references to cannabis,

or use related imagery. Rastafari imagery, a palm leaf image, and the words *'coffee shop'* have become the default signage.

> Restrictions could be placed on advertising for certain types of paraphernalia that contain drug references.

Location/density of outlets

> Zoning controls could be exercised by local licensing authority in a similar fashion to licensing of outlets for alcohol sales. Controls could also be exercised over size and type of outlets. This is the case in the Netherlands where, for example, some municipalities do not permit coffee shops (leading to some internal domestic *'drug tourism'*), and others have closed coffee shops near to schools. This latter seems excessive in a dense urban environment, and is probably more politically motivated— controls similar to those already used to manage bars/off licenses would be adequate in such cases.

Licensing of vendors/suppliers—general

> Broadly similar to licensing of commercial alcohol vendors/ licensees.

> Additional requirement for relevant health and safety training of vendors—for example, to restrict sales to those already intoxicated, offer advice on services, etc.

> Shared responsibility re: public nuisance in immediate environment, litter, local enforcement costs.

> Outlets would, initially at least, be limited to sale/consumption of cannabis only. In the Netherlands prohibition of sale of all other drugs, including alcohol, is a non-negotiable licence condition.

> All vendors would be required to promote responsible, safer use, and prominently provide drug information and information on relevant drug services.

> Venues also offering food or live music would come under the same local regulatory infrastructure, security and health and safety requirements.

> Permitted hours of opening would be determined by the local licensing authority.

> The Dutch coffee shops are restricted to holding less than 300g on the premises

at anytime. This is largely designed to control illicit *'back door'* supply; such limits would probably not be necessary for licensed premises under a legal regulated production scenario.

Volume sales/rationing controls

> Restrictions on bulk sales could be put in place, establishing a reasonable threshold for personal use. A 5g limit operates in the Netherlands. There is nothing to prevent multiple purchasing from different outlets; however, the general ease of cannabis availability means that such multiple purchasing is a marginal issue.

CONTROLS OVER THE PURCHASER/USER

Age access controls

> Vendors would be required to enforce age controls though an ID system—precise age of access would be locally determined but they would likely be in line with local alcohol and tobacco access age limits. In the Netherlands the age limit for coffee shops is 18.

Degree of intoxication of purchaser.

> Vendors would be required to refuse sales to those clearly intoxicated according to a clear set of guidelines. Drunkenness would be the most obvious concern.

LICENCES FOR PURCHASERS/USERS

> The Netherlands' experience suggests that licences to buy are probably unnecessary. However, they might usefully be deployed in certain scenarios, either as part of an incremental roll out process, or where specific problems arose. For example, in the Netherlands a residents only condition on sale is being introduced in some locations to deal with cross border trade issues, and there has also been recent discussion about making coffee shops members only.

Limitations in allowed locations for consumption

> Zoning laws familiar from alcohol control could designate public spaces, or areas with potential public order issues, as non-smoking areas. These laws would support

and build on local ordinances concerning public intoxication or disorderly conduct.

> Pre-existing restrictions on smoking in indoor public spaces would also apply to cannabis smoking.[64] As with tobacco, smoking in public venues could only take place on open air terraces or similar. Such a prohibition, involving civil or administrative sanction rather than a criminal offence, could be used to encourage less harmful forms of cannabis consumption. Vaporisers—which do not generate smoke and are not associated with the specific smoke related cannabis risks—could be exempted from no-smoking ordinances.[65]

Further reading

* R. Room *et al.*, *'The Global Cannabis Commission Report'*, The Beckley Foundation, 2007
* *'Cannabis Policy, Implementation and Outcomes'*, RAND Europe, 2003
* M. Aoyagi, *'Beyond Punitive Prohibition: Liberalizing the Dialogue on International Drug Policy'*, (includes detailed discussion of Dutch cannabis policy and law), 2006
* *'Cannabis'*, EMCDDA drug profile

5.4   **Stimulants**

This section focuses on the three most widely used types of currently illicit stimulants—amphetamines, cocaine and MDMA/ecstasy.

Potential stimulant regulation models need to respond appropriately to the risks presented by this group of drugs. So, it is important to acknowledge that use behaviours encompass a broad spectrum of motivations, environments and product preparations. These are associated with a

---

64 A curious situation has emerged in the Netherlands where anti-tobacco smoking ordinances have collided with coffee shop licensing. This has meant that cannabis smoking is legal whilst tobacco smoking is not—leading to the peculiar scene of local enforcers checking joints being smoked for prohibited tobacco content.

65 Vancouver, Canada, has one such *'vaporizer lounge'* in which smoking is not allowed.

wide range of risks and harms, all presenting very different regulatory challenges. However, they can be divided up into three broad categories:

* **Functional**—sometimes crossing over into medical use, and perhaps more usefully coming under the heading of *'lifestyle drugs'*. For example, users might be seeking to stave off tiredness, or aid concentration.

* **Recreational**—users seeking stimulation and enjoyment in a wide range of social contexts.

* **Problematic**—for a small minority of the functional or recreational users, stimulant use evolves into problematic/ dependent use. Such issues are most commonly associated with higher potency preparations (for example, crack cocaine, methamphetamine) and/or more risky patterns of rapid release consumption—that is, smoking and injection, as opposed to oral use or snorting.

It should also be noted that much of contemporary culture and society is steeped in stimulants. Pharmaceutical stimulants are widely prescribed and consumed in vast quantities (including, controversially, by children[66]). In addition, two of the world's favourite psychoactive drugs, nicotine and caffeine, are functional stimulants; between them, they saturate much of contemporary culture to the point of ubiquity.

Caffeine, in the number one spot, is most commonly consumed in the form of coffee, cola drinks and chocolate. Caffeine based *'energy drinks'* are also becoming increasingly popular. They are aggressively marketed specifically on the basis of their stimulant properties, much like tobacco and amphetamines used to be. Such drinks are a very clear indicator of caffeine consumption's key driver. It is valued primarily for its functional stimulant properties, rather than for pleasure or recreation *per se*. It scores low on any rational drug harm

66 See: N. Gibbs, *'The Age of Ritalin'*, TIME magazine, June 24, 2001.

assessment, but is none the less demonstrably not risk-free. Its use is, however, largely unregulated.

Caffeine's widespread non-harmful—indeed, largely beneficial—consumption is mirrored in the widespread use of low potency cocaine preparations; for example, coca leaf chewing and coca tea in the Andean regions of South America. It should be noted that the legality of this remains contentious in international law (see: page 34). Similar localised patterns of stimulant use exist elsewhere, including khat use in Somali speaking Africa, and betel nut use in South Asia and the Pacific. These are both associated with more clearly documented public health concerns than coca or caffeine drinks, but remain legal in their respective locales.

There is a significant set of behaviours that involves recreational stimulant use in social contexts. These behaviours are driven either by the pleasure of stimulant use itself, or as a quasi-functional adjunct to a social behaviour. Such functional motivations include staying awake into the night, enhancing confidence and alertness in social interactions, providing the energy to dance for longer, and so on. Inevitably this involves higher dosage, although generally less frequent, consumption than more obviously functional/lifestyle use. As such, it presents a different set of risks and challenges—not least because the user population is largely made up of young people.

Among these populations there is considerable flexibility in stimulant using behaviours. They can be easily substituted depending on taste or availability, and are often used in combination. Even though such patterns of use present increased risk levels, they are for the most part not associated with significant personal or social harms.[67] Use is generally occasional, moderate and contained by social norms that emerge amongst using and non-using peer groups in a social context. These norms are further tempered by personal controls, based on both experience and informed understanding of usage risks.

Key regulatory challenges for recreational stimulant using populations will include risk reduction and preventing progression to problematic/dependent use. Movement towards lower risk products and preparations (lower dose, slower release, orally administered), more informed and lower risk using behaviours (moderation—including abstinence—avoiding poly-drug use/bingeing, supporting peers, etc.), and stimulant use in safer environments should also be encouraged.

Finally there is the subset of the above users who will progress into chaotic, dependent or otherwise problematic stimulant use. Such behaviour is often concurrent with problematic use of other non-stimulant drugs, commonly including opiates and alcohol. For these populations, the most effective response is more medically orientated. In particular, it requires regulated supply models to focus on harm reduction (essentially as described above), combined with appropriate provision of treatment/recovery services, plus relevant holistic social support.

5.4.1 Cocaine/coca products

Coca/cocaine based drugs vary dramatically in nature, and thus in risk level. Different preparations run from negligible-risk orally consumed coca leaf and coca tea, through moderate-risk snorted cocaine powder (the salt of cocaine; cocaine-hydrochloride), to high-risk smoked crack (cocaine base). These are discussed below in reverse order.

Cocaine related risks and harms are also significantly determined by using behaviours. A detailed global study of cocaine use undertaken by the World Health Organization and UN Inter-regional Crime and Justice Research Institute (UNICRI) in 1995[68] noted that:

It is not possible to describe an 'average cocaine user'. An enormous

---

68 The WHO/UNICRI, '*The Cocaine Project*' report was suppressed following pressure from the US—only later being leaked into the public domain; another example of politics interfering with the drug and drug policy research agenda (see: *Appendix 2*, page 203, for more discussion). It is available online here: www.tdpf.org.uk/WHOleaked.pdf.

variety was found in the types of people who use cocaine, the amount
of drug used, the frequency of use, the duration and intensity of use,
the reasons for using and any associated problems they experience.
(page 1)

The report describes a continuum of using behaviours:

* *experimental use*
* *occasional use*
* *situation-specific use*
* *intensive use*
* *compulsive/dysfunctional use*

> *Experimental and occasional use are by far the most common*
> *types of use, and compulsive/dysfunctional is far less common.*
> (page 28)

And notes that:

> *Health problems from the use of legal substances, particularly*
> *alcohol and tobacco, are greater than health problems from cocaine*
> *use. Few experts describe cocaine as invariably harmful to health.*
> *Cocaine-related problems are widely perceived to be more common*
> *and more severe for intensive, high-dosage users and very rare and*
> *much less severe for occasional, low-dosage users.* (page 6)

Crack cocaine

The question *'but what about crack?'* is never far away when legal regulation of cocaine is discussed. It is an important and reasonable point to
pursue. Problematic crack users are at the hard end of chaotic drug use,
and cause a disproportionate amount of secondary harms to society.
Given this, how do we manage or attempt to regulate a drug like crack

cocaine, which is most associated with uncontrolled use, chaos and danger? The answer, as elsewhere, is to begin by moving beyond over-simplified solutions that have, over the years, demonstrably failed to produce effective outcomes.

Despite the best efforts of criminal justice enforcement, and others engaged in conventional prevention, crack dependence is a problem that has not been eradicated. Given this, we need to accept the reality that some people want to and will use crack, however distasteful such an acceptance may be. Then, we need to consider all available evidence. This will help us understand what kinds of intervention will be most effective at reducing the harm that crack use causes both to users, and to the wider community. Such harm reduction should of course include both a longer term reduction in overall crack use, and in the size of the using population.

We should be under no illusion that crack presents one of the most diffi-cult challenges for proponents of a legal regulatory model. However, the pragmatic reality remains that if someone is determined enough to use crack, they will do so. It therefore seems logical that, rather than sourcing it through an illicit marketplace, with all its attendant risks and harms, crack users should have legal access to a supply of known strength and purity. Such legal access will ensure that users do not have to commit crimes against others, or prostitute themselves, as a means of obtaining it.

Given this, it would seem that future approaches should start with the proposition that there is no benefit in further criminalising and demo-nising crack users. Instead, a concerted public health-led response, combined with appropriate social support, would seem to be a more productive response to a so far intractable issue. Whilst regulation has an important role to play in reducing harm, it is clear that addressing the social conditions and low levels of wellbeing that underlie most problematic use of crack, and other drugs, is the key to reducing such harmful behaviours in the longer term.

Public health responses are more difficult and less well established for crack than for heroin. While even the most chaotic heroin users will respond to regular prescriptions that satisfy their needs, crack users will often binge frequently and uncontrollably. While heroin users may accept substitute prescriptions such as methadone, no such alternatives for crack exist. Research continues into a range of possibilities, including prescription of substitute stimulants[69] such as amphetamines and Modafinil, or use of less potent cocaine preparations.[70] This is clearly an area of research that requires substantially more attention and investment.

The need for such research is becoming increasingly urgent as the growing concurrent use of crack and heroin makes managing crack related issues more and more difficult. Arguably, this development in crack usage is another unintended consequence of prohibition. It has been driven by the supply infrastructure and underground culture that has grown up around the illicit opiate market—a market and a culture that legalisation and consequent regulation would actively and directly help dismantle.

Crack could of course be prohibited, but regulation frameworks should also acknowledge that if powder cocaine is available—either legally or illicitly on sale, or on prescription—then crack is effectively available too. Making crack from powder cocaine is a simple kitchen procedure, and one that is impossible to prevent. Even if crack were not directly available, determined users previously willing to enter a dirty and dangerous illegal market to procure it would clearly not lack the motivation to manufacture it from a legal powder cocaine supply.

More positively, basic crack harm reduction methods are becoming reasonably well established. For example, Vancouver is one of a number of locations that distributes crack harm reduction kits, and some tentative experiments have also begun with supervised consumption venues for crack use.[71] These interventions point towards a model in which,

69 A useful summary: Kampman, 'The search for medications to treat stimulant dependence', Addiction Science and Clinical Practice, 4(2), 2008, pages 28–35.

70 WHO/UNICRI, 'The Cocaine Project' report, 1995, page 16.

71 'Distributing safer crack use kits in Canada', Canadian HIV Legal Network, 2008.

although crack might not be available directly, harm reduction provision would be made for those who continued to procure and use it, regardless of whether they do so through illicit or quasi-licit channels.

This kind of legally accessible cocaine powder/supervised crack consumption venue model creates clear potential for reductions in the personal and social harms created by the current illicit crack market. These reductions are of sufficient magnitude to outweigh the potential increase in health harms that might result for some users from a lowering of the cost availability barrier that constrains crack use for lower income chaotic users. It is also worth noting that, even for the most chaotic of those users, crack use is not infinite. It is limited by physiological factors, as well as by cost constraints.

There are also clear lessons to be learned from historic provision of heroin and other opiate prescribing and harm reduction services such as supervised injecting venues. Lessons from these experiences suggest that engaging directly and constructively with problem users' immediate needs, through harm reduction or other service provision, has a very clearly defined positive impact. In particular, it increases the likelihood that they will not only use drugs more safely and moderately, and do so in a safer peer environment, but that they will also come into contact with, and be more likely to utilise the wider service provisions on offer.

The *'what about crack?'* question is also one that highlights the role of prohibition in the emergence of the *'crack epidemic'*. Prohibition creates unregulated markets, driven by very clearly defined economic processes.[72] One effect of these is to encourage the creation and use of more potent drugs or concentrated drug preparations, which are more profitable per unit weight. This is directly comparable to the way that, under alcohol prohibition, the trade in beer and wines gave way to sales of more concentrated, profitable and dangerous spirits. This same

72 See: J. Miron, *'Drug War Crimes'*, The Independent Institute, 2004, page 16.

pattern has been observed over the past century in a variety of different illicit drug markets. For example, in opiate marketplaces, opium (either smoked or served in drinkable form) has been replaced by injectable heroin. More recently, the illegal cannabis market has become increasingly saturated with more potent indoor-grown varieties.

With coca-based products the transformation has been dramatic. Before its prohibition, the most popular forms of cocaine use were low-risk coca leaf chewing and coca-based tea and wine drinks. Snorted cocaine powder was first introduced onto the streets as a result of the demands of prohibition created illicit markets. These same market pressures finally led to the development and emergence of high-risk smokable crack.

It is notable that the market for cocaine (outside of the Andean regions) is currently defined by the fact that only the strongest and most risky forms of the drug are available. If less potent preparations were available, demand would be likely to move away from the more risky preparations, just as patterns of alcohol use shifted back towards beers and wines when US alcohol prohibition was repealed. This is especially the case if the regulatory gradients described in *chapter 3*, page 39, were applied with this specific aim.

In the case of crack cocaine in the UK, the long-established illegal heroin market created a ready made distribution network and receptive user base for the new product. The heroin and crack markets have meshed within a comparatively short period—most crack users are also heroin users. If these illegal networks were dismantled through the introduction of regulated supply, the next new drug *'epidemic'* would be far less likely to take hold.

Proposed discussion model for regulation of cocaine powder

BASIC REGULATORY MODELS

> Cocaine-hydrochloride powder would be available to licensed users under a retail specialist pharmacist model, or under some limited circumstances, medical prescription.

> Supply would either be entirely state controlled or via a state licensed entity under tender (see: *Regulated Market Model*, page 27).

CONTROLS OVER THE PRODUCT

Dosage and preparation

> The powder would be a pharmaceutical grade product (subject to the same controls as medicines).

> On the basis that pure cocaine is almost unknown on the illicit market, a legal product could potentially be reduced to an appropriate purity level below 100% through use of a safe, non toxic cutting agent.

> Microtaggants could be included under certain scenarios—(see below).

Price controls

> Fixed unit prices or minimum/maximum prices could be specified—with taxation potentially included on a per unit weight or % basis.

> The precise level of prices would have to be varied based on cautious experimentation and close monitoring of key outcomes over time (re levels of use and responses of illicit market—see: discussion of drug pricing, page 41).

> Initially they would be set at a point marginally below illicit market prices (Haden[73] has suggested around 70% as a starting point for legal stimulant pricing).

> Under a licensed user/purchase tracker model prices could potentially increase with volume of purchase as a disincentive to excessive use.

Packaging controls

> Non-branded plain packaging—as per medical drugs.

73 Mark Haden, '*Controlling illegal stimulants: a regulated market model*', Harm Reduction Journal, 2008, 5:1.

> Powder would be in fixed unit sealed sachets which would be provided within a secondary sealed container.

> The container would be tamper proof and child proof.

> Standard labelling—contents (strength/potency), units, health and safety, use by dates etc. Summary information and prominent warnings on containers and sachets would be augmented by a more detailed printed information insert in the container.

> Licensed purchaser details could be on both container and unit sachets as appropriate.

CONTROLS OVER THE VENDOR/SUPPLY OUTLET

Licensing of vendors/suppliers—general

> See: *2.2.4 Pharmacy model,* page 23, for more discussion.

> Permitted hours of opening, density/location of outlets would be determined by local licensing authority.

Advertising/promotion

> Total ban on all advertising and promotion—including strict controls on appearance/ signage of outlets.

Volume sales/rationing controls

> There would need to be a realistic acceptance that some degree of sharing would take place in social settings, even if sales are volume limited for personal use only. Volume of sales per purchaser (per day/week/month) would correspondingly have an upper limit established (and/or escalating price/volume structure).

> Potential for individual purchasers to be licensed, requiring an ID linked to a central purchase tracking database to enforce rationing controls.

CONTROLS OVER THE PURCHASER/USER

Age access controls

> ID enforced age controls—potentially linked to licensed purchaser system.

Degree of intoxication of purchaser

> Vendors would be required to refuse sales to those clearly intoxicated—according to a clear set of guidelines.

Licences for purchasers/users

> In the first instance at least (certainly for pilot schemes) a system would be established under which only licensed individuals would be allowed access for personal use only. This could be linked to an ID based purchase tracker system. Licences could be revoked for specified violations (e.g. secondary sales).

> Purchasers could have details of the named buyer encoded on packaging (or through use of microtaggants).

Limitations in allowed locations for consumption

> Public consumption would be a fineable offence in most locations.

> Particular attention should be given to highlighting the risks associated with cocaine consumption in conjunction with alcohol.

Potential models for regulation of lower strength cocaine preparations

As already highlighted, coca tea has a usage and public health profile in the Andean regions not dissimilar to that of coffee and conventional tea in much of the rest of the world. There is no reason why it could not be made more widely available on a similar basis, for those who desire it.[74] Its use in the short to medium term would be likely to remain largely within its cultural homeland. On an international level, it would probably find most market share in the speciality tea market. There is no particular reason to think it would replace or seriously encroach on coffee and tea markets where they are established.

74 In reality it is already widely available, yet the international market remains small.

More likely is that entrepreneurs might seek to develop new coca based *'energy drinks'* to compete with the lucrative caffeine based soft drink market. The most obvious template for such drinks would be existing cola drinks. They might also compete in the substantial, and rapidly growing higher caffeine content *'energy drinks'* market, sharing shelf space with products like Red Bull. Whilst coca tea has a natural limit to its active content, processed beverages would not. They would therefore have to be subject to additional tiers of regulation, so that active content could be controlled and limited, appropriate information incorporated into labelling and packaging, and other appropriate controls with regards to advertising/promotions established.

Such drinks would presumably (depending on active content levels and related risk assessments) be made available under a licensed sales model similar to that governing alcohol sales. Alternatively, they might only be available over the counter in pharmacies, as Red Bull is in certain European countries. Of course, such regulation might not just cover coca based drinks; there is a strong case that the packaging, promotion and availability of some caffeine based energy drinks should also be more strictly regulated.[75]

Such coca based beverages have the potential to absorb some of the user demand for cocaine powder. Many recreational consumers, if given a choice, would prefer a stimulant beverage that has a safer, slower release effect than that of a snorted powder. This preference could be further encouraged by using pricing and availability controls to make coca based energy beverages more attractive than snorted powder alternatives.

Such a development could both be a beneficial form of risk reduction, and potentially contribute to a more moderate and responsible culture of stimulant consumption—a culture which has, in the past few decades, moved in the opposite direction. Regulators would, however, need to consider the particular risks of such products being consumed

---

75 Such calls have increasingly come from a variety of medical authorities. See: C. Reissig, E. Strain, R. Griffiths, *'Caffeinated energy drinks—a growing problem'*, Drug and Alcohol Dependence, January 1, 2009.

in combination with other drugs—particularly alcohol. They should be aware, for example, how cocaine use has been associated with problematic patterns of drinking.

Illustrating this potential concern is the rise of caffeine-based energy drink/alcohol spirit cocktails in some markets. The popular Red Bull and vodka cocktail is perhaps the most visible example of this. Some pre-mixed combination beverage products have also emerged which cash in on this caffeine/alcohol cocktail trend. Such cocktails are problematic because the stimulant/depressant effects of their component drugs can, to some degree, cancel each other out. This can lead to excessive consumption, and thus increased risk. An additional concern around the potential for coca/alcohol cocktails is that co-administration of cocaine and alcohol leads to the formation of cocaethylene within the body. This is a drug with similar properties to cocaine; it is, however, thought to have higher cardiovascular and liver toxicity.

Regulatory models could respond to these concerns with a combination of availability restrictions and risk education. These could include restrictions on the sale of coca based drinks over a given strength in alcohol off-licences and bars, limiting such drinks to over-the-counter pharmacy sales only, prohibiting pre-mixed combination drinks or cocktails, enforcing specific warnings on packaging, and placing appropriate controls on advertising, promotion and branding.

Other oral coca/cocaine products

According to the 1995 WHO/UNICRI study, the traditional consumption of the coca leaf, chewed with a small quantity of lime to release the active contents:

> ...appears to have no negative health effects and has positive, therapeutic, sacred and social functions for indigenous Andean populations.

Many of coca leaf's functional and beneficial uses in Andean indigenous communities are quite regionally and culturally specific. For example, it helps combat altitude sickness, and delivers certain locally beneficial nutrients. As such, it seems relatively unlikely that there would be a substantial market for traditional Andean style coca leaf chewing in the wider world, even if no legal obstacles to its production and export existed. Other culturally/regionally specific stimulants such as khat and betel nut have similarly not found significant wider markets.

However, since cocaine is absorbed far more efficiently through the palate than through the stomach, there might be potential for the development of more consumer friendly coca leaf based products. These might be comparable to oral tobacco products, like *'Bandits'*. A quantity of coca leaf, plus an alkali additive, could be contained in a permeable, tea bag-like pouch, which would sit inside the mouth. Coca based products could also take the form of lozenges or chewing gums, to be consumed much like current similar nicotine substitution products. Such products would require levels of regulation appropriate to the levels of risk they present. These are, however, assumed to be relatively low; such products would probably require levels of regulation akin to comparable nicotine replacement products.

Were such products to emerge they would generally sit within the functional/beneficial/lifestyle arenas of stimulant using behaviours. They would presumably not have a significant impact on recreational or problematic patterns of use[76] beyond, arguably, helping foster a culture of more moderate, sensible use. As with non smoked tobacco products, however, regulators and public health officials have often struggled to reconcile the active promotion of such new products with their public health principles, which emphasise reduced use (see: *Tobacco harm reduction*, page 108). A clear case can be made that oral tobacco products are dramatically safer substitutes for smoked tobacco. However, the extent of a similar substitution with cocaine products is not established.

---

76 The 1995 WHO/UNICRI Cocaine Project report does mention the possibility of using coca tea for dependent cocaine users with some positive outcomes (page 16).

Introducing low strength oral coca products could effectively be creating a new market niche and behaviour where none existed.

On the other hand, such products are likely to emerge in some form under a new legal regime, and thus at least warrant consideration. Additionally, their emergence may merely serve to expand consumer choice between products, such as tobacco/nicotine or coffee, that serve a similar function and cultural role.

5.4.2 **Amphetamines**

There are a number of related drugs that come under the amphetamine grouping. Amphetamine itself (the name derived from its full chemical name: alpha-methylphenethylamine) is the parent compound for a large number of derivatives, each with a slightly different molecular forma-tion, of which there are four main types:

* Amphetamine; racemic variation; dextroamphetamine (Dexedrine)
* Methyl-amphetamine; racemic variation dexmethamphetamine (more commonly known as just methamphetamine)
* Ketoamphetmaines; cathine and cathinone (the active ingredients in khat)
* Pseudo-amphetamines; methylphenidate (Ritalin) etc.

MDMA (ecstasy) is another amphetamine related substance, dealt with separately below.

Across the globe, amphetamines are the second most popular illegal drug after cannabis.[77] They are, like cocaine, associated with a spectrum of using behaviours and preparations that span from functional/medical, through recreational, to problematic. These behaviours are correspond-ingly associated with a wide spectrum of risks and regulatory challenges.

As with other drug groupings there is a need to balance the short term needs to reduce the harm associated with more harmful or risky forms of use with the longer term goal of progressively shifting use towards safer products, behaviours and environments. This might include provision of more risky preparations, such as powders or injectable forms, only under much more restrictive regimes.

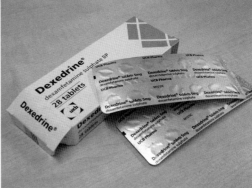

Medically prescribed Dexedrine tablets (dexamphetamine sulphate)

FLICKR/FGMB

The usefulness of amphetamines for a range of medical applications—from over the counter nasal decongestants and cold remedies,[78] to treatments for attention-deficit hyperactivity disorder and narcolepsy—means that, unlike cocaine, many amphetamines are in wide legal circulation in a number of forms. This means that they are both more accessible (including diversion/conversion for non-medical use), and their risks, use and misuse are arguably better understood and accommodated, both medically and socially.

Proposed discussion model for regulation of amphetamine

BASIC REGULATORY MODELS

> Dexamphetamine (and potentially some other amphetamines)—would be available in pill form under the specialist pharmacist model only—initially under a licensed purchaser model.

> A powder form could potentially also be available under some scenarios—with stricter availability controls.

> Weaker preparations, including oral solutions, could be available over the counter or under an appropriate licensed sales system—subject to volume sales restrictions.

> A medical prescription model would exist in parallel to any licensed retail supply.

---

78 Which sometimes contain levomethamphetamine and pseudoephedrine.

CONTROLS OVER THE PRODUCT

Dosage and preparation

> Any pill and powder form drugs would be produced and sold under standard pharmaceutical drug controls.

> Pills could be formulated to prevent/discourage crushing for snorting/injecting.

> Dosage would be standardised at an appropriate level, on a per pill or powder sachet basis (determined by experience with prescribed amphetamines).

> Like cocaine, any powder form amphetamines for snorting could be reduced in potency below 100%, with the addition of non-toxic cutting agents.

> The use of slow release dermal patches, already used for methylphenidate (Ritalin), could also be explored.

Price controls

> Fixed unit prices or minimum/maximum prices could be specified, with taxation included on a per unit weight or % basis.

> An increasing price/tax gradient could be introduced, from lower dose slower release to higher dose faster release preparations.

> Prices would likely be similar or marginally lower than current illicit market prices. Amphetamine prices are, however, generally relatively low anyway and are correspondingly less of a factor in using decisions. A reduction in price could thus serve to undermine illicit production and supply without necessarily encouraging use. As with all drug pricing, developments would have to be based on cautious experimentation and close monitoring of key outcomes.

Packaging controls

> Non-branded plain packaging—as per medical drugs.

> Pills would be in standardised medical drug pill bottles/containers, or blister packs within appropriate container. Powder would be in fixed unit sachets or wraps, which would be provided within a sealed container.

> Containers would be tamper proof and child proof.

> Standard labelling—contents (strength/potency), units, health and safety, use by
> dates, etc. Summary information and prominent warnings on containers (and
> wraps/sachets) could be augmented by a more detailed printed information insert
> in the container. Labelling would prominently specify *'not for medical use'* to help
> maintain the market distinction between medical and non-medical supply.

> Licensed purchaser details could be on both container and unit sachets/blister packs,
> as appropriate.

CONTROLS OVER THE VENDOR/SUPPLY OUTLET

Advertising/promotion

> All advertising and promotion would be prohibited for pill and powder form
> amphetamines, including strict controls on appearance/signage of outlets.

> Some promotion of lower strength/over the counter products (weak oral solutions
> and *'energy drinks'*) could be permitted under strict conditions, as already happens
> with some legal amphetamine products.

Licensing of vendors/suppliers—general

> See pharmacy model for more discussion.

> Permitted hours of opening, density/location of outlets would be determined by local
> licensing authority.

Volume sales/rationing controls

> Volume of sales per purchaser (per day/week/ month) would have an upper limit
> established (and/or an escalating volume/price structure) that would be set at a
> realistic level for personal use (once weekly/four times a month perhaps), but well
> below what would be seen as problematic level/frequency (i.e. daily use). There would
> need to be a realistic acceptance that some degree of sharing would take place in social
> settings—even if sales are limited and on the purchaser/personal use only basis.

> Problematic/dependency levels of use would be managed through a medical prescription model.

> Rationing controls could be enforced through use of individual purchaser licensing linked to ID based purchase tracking.

CONTROLS OVER THE PURCHASER/USER

Age access controls

> Vendors would be required to enforce age controls through checking ID—potentially linked to a licensed purchaser system.

Degree of intoxication of purchaser

> Vendors would be required to refuse sales to those clearly intoxicated, according to a clear set of guidelines.

Licences for purchasers/users

> In the first instance at least (certainly for pilot schemes) a system would be established under which only licensed individuals would be allowed access for personal use only. This could be linked to an ID based purchase tracker system. Licences could be revoked for specified offences, such as secondary sales.

> Purchases could have details of the named buyer encoded on packaging, or through use of microtaggants.

Limitations in allowed locations for consumption

> Public consumption in pill form would not be an issue; public snorting could be a fineable offence in most locations.

> The risks associated with consuming amphetamines in conjunction with alcohol should be strongly highlighted.

Other amphetamines:

Methylphenidate (Ritalin)

Ritalin is widely prescribed to treat a variety of medical conditions. Its best known—and most controversial—use is as a treatment for attention deficit hyperactivity disorder, in school and even preschool children.[79] It has also been widely diverted for non-medical stimulant use; the prevalence of medical use by children has led to particular misuse issues within that group. Development of slower release one-a-day preparations and transdermal patches have gone some way to addressing this diversion issue.

However, while remaining a serious concern, the issues around prescription diversion amongst children should not affect potential non-medical access by consenting adults. Where legal access to dexamphetamine existed, demand for other diverted medical amphetamines with similar effect profiles, like Ritalin, would naturally diminish. Should any demand remain, a regulated supply of non-medical methylphenidate could be made available in parallel, or even instead of, dexamphetamine, on a similar basis.

Methamphetamine

Methamphetamine is a more potent and long acting amphetamine, although its distinction from other amphetamines has probably been overstated—the key distinctions being its ease of production, and the fact that it can be more easily smoked (see: *4.2 Assessing Drug Harms*, page 70). Over the last two decades, as its medical uses have diminished, its illicit non-medical production and use have grown rapidly. It has become a major public health concern in a number of regions, notably south-east Asia, Eastern Europe, the Russian Federation and North America.

---

[79] Dexamphetamine and Adderal (a mix of Ritalin and dexamphetamine) have also been widely prescribed for this condition.

In the absence of legally accessible options for other amphetamines or stimulants, profiteers have once again been able to skew illicit markets towards the most potent, risky and profitable products

As a result, and combined with substantial problems associated with the drugs illicit trade, methamphetamine has become very much the *'new drug menace'*. In the US, for example, it has, to some extent, assumed the status in the drug war narrative formerly occupied by crack cocaine. As a result, media panic has generated hyperbolic accounts of the threat that it represents. It is important that such hyperbole obscures neither a realistic understanding of the serious usage-related problems facing a significant minority of its users, nor the fact that much of its use is largely non-problematic. It should also be acknowledged that methamphetamine is easily manufactured from accessible precursor chemicals and drugs, which include over the counter medicines (ephedrine and pseudoephedrine). This at once makes control next to impossible, and creates an attractive and lucrative market for criminal profiteers. In the absence of legally accessible options for other amphetamines or stimulants, such profiteers have once again been able to skew illicit markets towards the most potent, risky and profitable products.[80]

In regions where methamphetamine has become a major problem, separate but parallel responses are required to address the challenges it presents. In the short term there is a need to accept the realities of methamphetamine use as it currently exists, and to adopt public health-led approaches that reduce its associated personal health and social risks/harms. This would mirror the approach defined for crack cocaine above, with restricted provision, supervised use venues, and treatment/recovery/support services made available for problematic users.

Such harm reduction could be combined with maintenance prescription supply, where specific criteria were met. This would be managed according to established amphetamine prescription models. There may be some potential for prescription of less potent slow-release

---

80 In contrast to the US experience, in the UK, where illicit amphetamine sulphate is relatively cheap and accessible, methamphetamine use has remained very low.

amphetamines to problematic methamphetamine users.[81] These could be provided as weaker, slower release oral preparations, which would discourage higher risk smoking or injecting behaviours.

In the longer term, amphetamine and broader stimulant regulation would look to reverse the pressures created by illicit market economics. It would aim to nurture more personally healthy, and less socially harmful, relationships with stimulants. Regulatory tools would combine with public health education and harm reduction interventions to create a gradual, positive impact on stimulant users and stimulant using culture, progressively moving towards less risky drugs, preparations, behaviours and using environments.

Ephedrine

Ephedrine is similar both in chemical structure and effects to dexamphetamine and methamphetamine, although it is less potent than both. The drug occurs naturally in the ephedra plant, long used as a traditional Chinese medicine. Ephedrine is legally available in its hydrochloride and sulphate forms in many countries, including the US. It is sold both as a prescribed medicine and an over the counter pharmaceutical product, and is commonly used as a functional stimulant by professionals, students and some sportspeople.[82] Ephedrine also has other lifestyle/medical uses, including as a decongestant, appetite suppressant and bronchiodilator.

Until comparatively recently, ephedrine has had a relatively low profile among non-medical users. This changed when one of its isomers, pseudoephedrine, was found to be a primary precursor to methamphetamine. At this point, ephedrine became subject to increasingly restrictive controls. Interestingly, rather than absolute prohibition, the US responded by introducing a raft of strict regulations under the Combat Methamphetamine Epidemic Act of 2005,[83] which became law in 2006.

---

81 Studies using Methylphenidate for this purpose are underway in a number of countries including Finland and New Zealand.

82 Its safety for sports training is highly questionable and its legality in competitive sports is the subject of ongoing controversy.

83 For details, see: www.deadiversion.usdoj.gov/meth/index.html.

This amended the US Code concerning the sale of ephedrine-containing products. The federal statute included the following requirements for merchants who sell ephedrine or pseudoephedrine:

* A retrievable record of all purchases identifying the name and address of each party to be kept for two years.
* Required verification of proof of identity of all purchasers.
* Required protection and disclosure methods in the collection of personal information.
* Reports to the Attorney General of any suspicious payments or disappearances of the regulated products.
* Non-liquid dose form of regulated product may only be sold in unit dose blister packs.
* Regulated products are to be kept behind the counter or in a locked cabinet, in such a way as to restrict access.
* Daily sales of regulated products not to exceed 3.6 grams, without regard to the number of transactions.
* Monthly sales not to exceed 9 grams of pseudoephedrine base in regulated products—similar regulations apply to mail-order purchases, except the monthly sales limit is only 7.5 grams.

This response might seem to be at once rather draconian for the medicines and cold remedies that occupy most bathroom cabinets, and ineffectual at reducing the availability and use of illicit methamphetamine. Indeed, the production of methamphetamine has simply moved from small scale user-producers to a larger scale organised crime enterprise. However it does, if inadvertently, point towards some useful models of regulation for non-medical amphetamines.

5.4.3 Ecstasy/MDMA

MDMA—otherwise known as ecstasy—is a synthetic drug which is chemically similar to the amphetamines. However, its stimulant properties are complemented by other, very distinctive psychological effects that set it aside from other stimulants. These are described as creating a sense of empathy or intimacy in social situations. Ecstasy has accordingly been additionally referred to as an *'empathogen'* or *'entactogen'*.

Ecstasy/MDMA is by far the most popular of a large number of related psychoactive synthetic drugs (sometimes referred to as *'designer drugs'*) that have been developed over the last century.[84] None of the others (including 2CB and MDA) have achieved more than brief or relatively low level patterns of use within the illicit drug scene. Many, when they are observed, are in fact sold as ecstasy.

The rapid emergence of ecstasy into youth culture in the late 1980s and early 1990s was the spur for a familiar *'moral panic'*, which rumbles on sporadically to this day. This panic was accompanied by a growing body of research, assessing the risks and harms associated with the drug's use in a range of environments. There was a clear dissonance between this research and much of the political and media response to the panic, which tended to misrepresent population harms by focusing obsessively on individual fatalities.

The most recent and comprehensive, independent systematic review of the observational evidence[85] was published in 2009. It was a part of the UK's review of MDMA classification, undertaken by the government appointed Advisory Council on the Misuse of Drugs (ACMD). The 2009 ACMD report recommended that MDMA should be reclassified from (UK) class A to class B. In support of this, it noted that:

    ✢   *Use of MDMA is undoubtedly harmful. High doses may lead to death: by direct toxicity, in situations of hyperthermia/dehydration, excessive*

---

84 The most famous researcher being Alexander Shulgin who, in his book *'PiHKAL'* describes the process by which he developed and tested over 200 related substances, including MDMA (initially developed in 1912 by Merck).

85 G. Rogers *et al.*, *'The harmful health effects of recreational ecstasy: a systematic review of observational evidence'*, Health Technology Assessment, 2009; Vol. 13(6), pages 1–338. The study looked at over 4,000 published studies, 422 of which met the review criteria for inclusion.

water intake, or for other reasons. However, fatalities are relatively low given its widespread use, and are substantially lower than those due to some other Class A drugs, particularly heroin and cocaine. These risks can be minimised by following advice such as drinking appropriate amounts of water, although this is no substitute for abstinence.

* Some people experience acute medical consequences as a result of MDMA use, which can lead to hospital admission, sometimes with the requirement for intensive care. MDMA poisonings are not currently increasing in number and are less frequent than episodes due to cocaine.

* MDMA appears not to have a high propensity for dependence or withdrawal reactions, although a number of users seek help through treatment services.

* MDMA appears to have little acute or enduring effect on the mental health of the average user; unlike amphetamines and cocaine, it is seldom implicated in significant episodes of paranoia.

* There is presently little evidence of longer-term harms to the brain in terms of either its structure or function. However, there is evidence for some small decline in a variety of domains, including verbal memory, even at low cumulative dose. The magnitude of such deficits appears to be small and their clinical relevance is unclear. The evidence shows that MDMA has been misused in the UK for 20 years but it should be noted that long-term effects of use cannot be ruled out.

* Overall, the ACMD judges that the physical harms of MDMA more closely equated with those of amphetamine, than those of heroin or cocaine.

* MDMA use seems to have few societal effects in terms of intoxication related harms or social disorder. However, the ACMD notes a very small proportion of cases where 'ecstasy' use has been implicated in sexual assault.

*   *Dis-inhibition and impulsive, violent or risky behaviours are not commonly seen under the influence of MDMA, unlike with cocaine, amphetamines, heroin and alcohol.*

Key shortcomings in the research base should, of course, be acknowledged; MDMA is a relatively new drug (in widespread use) compared to, for example, amphetamine or cocaine, and its illegality is an additional research hindrance. However, we do now have a reasonable assessment of the drug's risks, specifically relative to other stimulants.

Its toxic/acute risks are *relatively* low, especially if basic risk reduction advice is followed; these include hydration, managing overheating issues in dance club venues/party environments, and being aware of poly-drug use risks. Whilst high risk use is observed, dependent patterns of use are extremely rare. Unlike cocaine and amphetamines, MDMA has neither functional/lifestyle low dose uses, nor the chronic dependence issues associated with high dose frequent usage.

Given this, we propose as a starting point a specialist pharmacist supply model, along the lines described for amphetamine and powder cocaine. MDMA's dance music/party scene use, might also mean that membership-based licensed club models could be explored, albeit on an experimental basis. This latter would be an appropriate response to an accepted reality of MDMA use; it is already easily and cheaply available in many club and related environments. In fact, the UK experience has been that costs per pill have dropped dramatically over the past two decades, although use has fallen marginally since its mid-90s peak. At a practical level, an on-site licensed outlet would facilitate informed choice on content and dosage. This informed choice is sacrificed in illicit markets, in which *'pills'* are of unknown strength, content and purity.

Licensed on-site vendors would also be able to assume many of the responsibilities of the pharmacist role. They would be expected to restrict sales on the basis of intoxication, multiple purchase and volume rationing, as well as offering advice on safer use. Such venues could initially be membership only. This would offer a degree of control over access, with removal of membership as sanction for any *'house rules'* violations. These could include sales to third parties, or supply to individuals who had already been denied club access.

In addition, MDMA's *'empathogen'*/*'entactogen'* properties could justify creating an additional channel of access: making the drug available for supervised therapeutic use via licensed medical practitioners. The use of MDMA in a range of therapeutic environments has been the subject of ongoing research into helping with couples therapy, depression, anxiety for cancer patients, and post traumatic stress. Without making any claims for its efficacy, such potentially beneficial research should not be curtailed purely on the basis of unrelated concerns about the drug's recreational use on the party scene. Acknowledging this, officially licensed research into the therapeutic uses of MDMA has begun to expand in the USA and elsewhere.[86]

5.4.4   Emerging MDMA analogues and other *'designer drugs'*

Over the past two or three decades, the emergence of MDMA, and a slew of related compounds, has raised some difficult questions about how public health and enforcement agencies deal with the emergence of new psychoactive drugs. In some countries, including the UK, entire categories of similar chemical compounds (including any variants potentially developed in the future) are covered by the same legislation.

It is reasonable to propose that any new drugs not covered by existing regulatory frameworks should not be, by default, legally available—as is often the case at present. A default prohibition, certainly on any form of commercial sales, would seem to be the more cautious and responsible course to take (poisons legislation could also come into play to cover

86 See for example: www.maps.org/mdma/.

distribution of unknown substances, especially if under misleading terms or without informed consent). Such a prohibition would exist until any such drug had been subject to appropriate evaluation and recommendations by the relevant regulatory agencies.

Quite how such a prohibition would operate raises a series of potentially tricky questions. Distinctions would have to be made, and sanctions determined, based on the nature of the drug and the motives for its production and supply. Commercial development and sales of unclassified drugs would be the key target of such a restriction. However, it seems likely that the incentive for illicit chemists to develop and market new drugs on an unregulated basis would diminish if licit alternatives were available. Such commercially driven activities would usefully be separated from the, admittedly marginal, activities of *'psychonauts'*— drug chemist/hobbyists. Research into new drugs would ideally take place within an academic or government body under some form of external supervision and scrutiny.

Further reading

* M. Haden, *'Controlling Illicit Stimulants: A Regulated Market Model'*, Harm Reduction Journal 5:1, 2008
* *'The Cocaine Project report'*, World Health Organization, and UN Inter-regional Crime and Justice Research Institute, 1995
* *'Coca Myths'*, Transnational Institute, 2009
* C. Reinarman, H. Levine (eds.), *'Crack in America: Demon Drugs and Social Justice'*, University of California Press, 1997
* M. Jay, *'From Soft Drink to Hard Drug; A Snapshot History of Coca, Cocaine and Crack'*, Transform Drug Policy Foundation, 2005
* T. Feiling, *'The Candy Machine: How Cocaine Took Over the World'*, Penguin, 2009
* P. Fleming, *'Prescribing amphetamine to amphetamine users as a harm reduction measure'*, International Journal of Harm

Reduction, 9:5, pages 339–344, 1998

❋   For background on different stimulant drugs see: the EMCDDA *'drug profiles'* resource: www.emcdda.europa.eu/publications/drug-profiles

❋   *'BZP: New Zealand's experiment with legal regulation of a non-medical stimulant'*, Transform Drug Policy Foundation, forthcoming

5.5   Psychedelics

The broad category of hallucinogens—that is, drugs that induce hallucinations—can usefully be broken down into three distinct subgroups, defined by mode of action and subjective effects. These subgroups are dissociatives,[87] deliriants,[88] and psychedelics. Here, we focus on psychedelics.

'Psychedelic' is a relatively new term—essentially meaning *'mind manifesting'*—used to describe a group of drugs that cause subjective changes in perception and consciousness. The psychedelics in most common non-medical usage are LSD (Lysergic Acid Diethylamide), psilocybin/psylocibe (natural plant form: *'magic'* mushrooms), mescaline (natural plant forms: peyote and San Pedro cacti) and DMT (natural plant form: ayahuasca).[89] Other drugs, including cannabis and some of the MDMA group, can have some psychedelic effects; these are not, however, the dominant effects, and thus these drugs are not included in the psychedelic grouping.

Whilst all have their own risk profiles, these psychedelics have a number of qualities in common. They are generally viewed as having low toxicity

---

[87] Dissociatives, including ketamine, PCP and nitrous oxide, tend to induce a sensory deprivation/out of body/lucid dreamlike experience by blocking the conscious mind from other parts of the mind (ketamine and nitrous oxide are used as anaesthetics because of these effects).

[88] Deliriants, including the mandrake, henbane and datura plants (and some pharmaceuticals at high doses including Benadryl) which have a specific mode of action in the brain and create profound hallucinations. They are also more toxic than other hallucinogens and often associated with unpleasant physical side effects—and are correspondingly not widely used recreationally (and have mostly never been prohibited), being of interest mostly to historians and a small group of 'psychonauts').

[89] Psychedelic drugs in plant form used in a religious or shamanic context are also sometimes described as 'entheogens'.

and potential for overdose. Fatalities associated with their use are correspondingly rare, and are usually either a result of poly-drug use, or accidents occurring under the influence due to lack of inhibitions, recklessness or disorientation.[90] These psychedelics are additionally not associated with patterns of dependent use (the intense nature of the experience being self limiting [91]) or withdrawal effects, and only rarely with frequent use or bingeing. It should, however, be noted that psychedelic use can be problematic in other ways. Key identified risks are the potentially serious exacerbation of pre-existing mental health problems, or precipitation of mental health problems that had previously gone undetected, and the potential for psychologically traumatic negative experiences (a 'bad trip'), occasionally including acute psychotic episodes.

Because of this low toxicity and low potential for dependence, most risk assessments of such psychedelics position them as low risk relative to most stimulant and depressant drugs.[92] The risks that do exist, which will inform the regulatory supply and use models proposed, are focused on those with particular mental health vulnerabilities, and issues around inappropriate set (mindset/emotional or psychological state when taking the drug) and setting (using environment—including physical and peer environment).

Use of psychedelics encompasses a range of behaviours. These can be broadly divided into use specifically for the drugs' 'mind manifesting' effects, as part of a planned personal or group exploration, experience, or ritual, and use more as an adjunct or enhancer of another recreational activity, in a variety of social settings—such as music concerts, parties, nightclubs and so on.

90 Whilst the high profile idea/meme that people under the influence of psychedelics might 'think they can fly and jump out of a window' is largely the result of the LSD panic of the 1960s, there have inevitably been some serious, occasionally fatal, accidents involving psychedelics.

91 Very rapid development of tolerance (including cross-tolerance between psychedelics) is another limiting factor.

92 See: Nutt *et al.*, 'Development of a rational scale to assess the harm of drugs of potential misuse', The Lancet, 369, 2007, pages 1047–1053. For historical reasons that can be traced back to the emergence of psychedelic drugs as a key part of the 1960s counter culture movement, the legal classifications (in the US and UK for example) tend to put psychedelics in the 'most harmful' categories—anomalously alongside heroin and cocaine.

Three of the four psychedelics discussed here, psilocybin, mescaline and DMT, occur in natural plant forms as well as processed pharmaceuticals. These plant based psychedelics have a long history of ritualised/sacramental/shamanic use in various cultures. Examples include the Native American sacramental use of peyote cactus, indigenous Andean use of San Pedro cactus, indigenous Amazonian use of ayahuasca, and the widespread use of psilocybin mushrooms, which reflects their geographical ubiquity.

The use of ayahuasca and peyote/San Pedro cacti outside of these localised indigenous cultures has been small scale and largely limited to a ritualised/spiritual context. The preparation of the plants for consumption is quite difficult and laborious, the brewed drinks that need to be consumed unpleasant, and in the case of ayahuasca, there are often side effects including vomiting and diarrhoea.[93] They have therefore, unsurprisingly perhaps, not become a feature of the recreational or party drug scene (unlike *magic* mushrooms—see below) and are only a marginal concern for regulation. Correspondingly, whilst the active drugs, mescaline and DMT, are prohibited, the plants themselves are generally not. Indeed, San Pedro cacti in particular is widely grown for ornamental use.

The current legal status of psychedelic drugs in plant form is somewhat ambiguous and confusing. This reflects the obvious practical problems of attempting to prohibit access to naturally occurring plants, or determining precise criteria for the point at which the owner of the plant/drug becomes the subject of punitive sanctions. While the 1971 UN Convention on Psychotropic Drugs includes mescaline, DMT and psilocine/psilosin in schedule 1, the commentary to the convention (the official guide to its implementation and use) makes it clear that:

> *The cultivation of plants from which psychotropic substances are obtained is not controlled by the Vienna Convention. (...) Neither*

---

93 Its sacramental use is often associated with a physical as well as spiritual cleansing process.

the crown (fruit, mescal button) of the Peyote cactus nor the roots of the plant Mimosa hostilis nor Psilocybe mushrooms themselves are included in Schedule 1, but only their respective principles, mescaline, DMT and psilocine, psilosin.

Article 32 of the 1971 convention itself does provide an additional exemption:

A State on whose territory there are plants growing wild which contain psychotropic substances from among those in Schedule 1 and which are traditionally used by certain small, clearly determined groups in magical or religious rites, may, at the time of signature, ratification or accession, make reservations concerning these plants, in respect of the provisions of article 7, except for the provisions relating to international trade.

A number of such exceptions have been implemented and exist in domestic law, providing a functioning legal model for ritual/sacramental use of psychedelics. One notable example of this is the permitted use of Peyote cactus/mescaline in the US by Native Americans, and the non-requirement for it to be declared on joining the military.

There are clearly lessons for wider regulatory models to be learnt from traditional ritual use. Such use operates within well established social/cultural controls, ensuring that use is only very occasional, and that set and setting are clearly delineated through careful ritualised preparation.

Under such a model, users are very well informed and organised; it is supported by mentoring and peer guidance, with a corresponding respect for the potentially profound and intense nature of the drug experience.

For users seeking the more exploratory psychedelic experience, a group/society/club type model could be based on some of the lessons of traditional ritual use. It would offer a wide range of psychedelics (potentially including LSD, and pharmaceutical preparations of DMT and Mescaline), and would combine elements of the licensed venue and vendor models with a licensed user/membership system.

Proposed discussion model for regulation of psychedelics

BASIC REGULATORY MODEL

> A membership based psychedelic group/club model that would combine elements of the specialist pharmacist model (a trained and licensed vendor with specific responsibilities), licensed premises for sale and consumption, and licensed users (a membership system with a requirement for training, and potentially meeting certain health criteria).

CONTROLS OVER THE PRODUCT

Dosage and preparation:

> For plant based psychedelics, quantifying dosage within acceptable error parameters would be based on established knowledge of quantities/effects for either drink preparations or—in the case of fresh or dried psilocybin mushrooms—weight, as appropriate to the potency of different species.

> Pharmaceutical preparations would be in standardised units at the lower end of the active dosage threshold—higher doses would be established in multiples or additional fractions of these units.

Price controls

> The existing illicit market for psychedelics is relatively small, with prices low enough, and use generally infrequent enough, for price to not be an important factor in using decisions—so the usefulness of price controls as a regulatory tool would be marginal.

> Fixed unit prices could be established with sales on a non-profit basis (even if other elements of the experience were charged for)—to reduce any profit incentive push

towards higher dosage/use, with potential for % or per-unit taxation. Operation of such groups on a not for profit basis would be preferable.

Packaging controls

> Supply of psychedelic drugs for use in licensed premises would not require specific packaging controls.

> Under a scenario where the drugs were taken off premises for any reason standard packaging controls would be mandated (see: page 45), including child and tamper proof containers, standardised labelling, and licensed user details as appropriate.

CONTROLS OVER THE VENDOR/SUPPLY OUTLET/PREMISES

Licensing of vendors/suppliers

The licensed vendors/venue licensees of the group/club would assume a number of roles and responsibilities including:

> A pharmacist-like role, providing information about effects, health and safety information, risk reduction, and services as well as limiting access under certain criteria (see user controls below). This would require standardised training as a condition of licence.

> Responsibility for monitoring wellbeing of users, and duty of care should they experience difficulties or problems—this might include a requirement for mentoring/guiding the experience/acting as a *'sitter'* (non-use being a prerequisite) particularly for first time or novice users. They might also be licensed to administer benzodiazepines, which dampen or negate intense psychedelic related distress.

> Safe/secure transit and storage of drug supplies, along with accurate record keeping of sales/members.

> Managing membership (inclusion and exclusion) according to clearly mandated criteria, and ensuring access was limited to members only.

> Enforcement of standard health and safety regulations.

> Restricting drug use within the group environment to specific licensed psychedelics.

Issues around venue location, density of outlets, and hours of opening would be determined by the local licensing authority but would not be a major issue as group or mentored use would be scheduled and venues could vary (including, for example, approved rented venues or private homes/gardens).

Volume sales/rationing controls

> If sales are for onsite supervised use, rationing is not an issue, as the drugs are dispensed for immediate use direct to the user by the vendor (consumption can be supervised).

> Any off site sales would be rationed at a level appropriate for personal occasional use.

CONTROLS OVER THE PURCHASER/USER

Age access controls

> Membership and access would have minimum age criteria (in all likelihood over 18).

Degree of intoxication/mindset of purchaser/user

> Vendors would be required to refuse sales to those clearly intoxicated, according to a clear set of guidelines.

> An additional restriction on access could be applied on a discretionary basis/to a set of established guidelines if the supplier viewed the prospective user's mindset to be non-conducive to a problem-free psychedelic experience, for whatever reason.

Licences/membership requirements for purchasers/users

> Access to membership of a psychedelic club/group could be conditional on participation in training sessions to establish a clear understanding of the potential positive and negative effects of different forms of psychedelic use, stressing the importance of set and setting, risks and responsibilities, etc.

> The membership system would aim to restrict/limit access to vulnerable individuals (those with certain mental health issues, emotional or psychological problems, or using potentially contra-indicated medications), for whom psychedelic use presented heightened or unacceptable levels of risk. How such criteria could be

objectively evaluated and implemented without being discriminatory or inconsistent is problematic; perhaps the best option would be for appropriate questions to be built into an informal membership interview (potentially also used to establish that training was adequate). Relevant information would, however, have to be volunteered (unless a requirement for a doctor's *'all clear'* was mandated).

> Potential for a tiered membership process; potentially beginning with a non-problematic supervised/guided/mentored lower dose/shorter acting drug experience, leading to *'graduation'* to extended access, if sought (by dosage/drugs). Once a member had established themselves as a responsible, informed and non-problematic user over a certain period they could then potentially graduate to being able to take out supplies for personal use.

> Membership/access could be revoked for violating group rules.

Pharmacy sales model

A licensed user/pharmacy-sales model could operate for certain psychedelics, potentially alongside a group model described above. This could either be for already established group members, or allow access based on a similar training/vetting process.

Lower threshold licensed sales for psilocybin (*'magic'*) mushrooms

Psilocybin or *'magic'* mushrooms are distinct from the other psyche-delics discussed here in some key respects. They are generally shorter acting[94] and, unlike peyote, San Pedro cacti and ayahuasca, they are consumable in their raw form without any preparation.[95] Thus, with some basic knowledge about potency, they offer relatively easy user-dosage control. In many parts of the world, they are available in the natural environment, and amongst the psychedelics they are generally

---

94 The effects commonly lasting 2–6 hours (depending on dosage and user) compared to 8–16 hours for mescaline, ayahuasca and LSD. An exception is the smoked pharmaceutical DMT which can last about 5–30 minutes.

95 They can also be made into a tea or prepared as food products.

regarded as least risky. The UK government's drug information website *'Frank'* notes that:

> *The biggest danger with taking any magic mushrooms is making sure you've picked the right thing. There are hundreds of varieties [of mushrooms] and some of them are highly poisonous.*[96]

This combination of factors means psilocybin mushrooms have a more obvious appeal than other psychedelics to the social user. This is reflected in their prevalence of use in this group. For example, usage has been rising over the past decade in Europe, becoming more popular than the previous favoured psychedelic, LSD. Psilocybin mushrooms are also used by a smaller population, usually in higher doses, for a range of more distinctly personal, exploratory, ritual and spiritual uses.

In a number of countries the ambiguous legal status of psilocybin mushrooms has meant they are or have been effectively legal for sale, subject only to voluntary regulation. They were, until a recent ban,[97] legally available in the Netherlands in so-called *'smart shops'*. For a number of years, they were only subject to voluntary regulation; age controls and some limited health and safety information appeared on the packaging. In the UK, when a legal loophole was identified in 2001–2 that allowed fresh psilocybin mushrooms to be sold legally, mushrooms imported from the Netherlands soon became widely available in *'head shops'*[98] and other outlets. They were subject to no formal regulation whatsoever, and were indeed often promoted and sold irresponsibly.[99] Somewhat predictably, this situation led to a more comprehensive ban in 2005.

Use of mushrooms rose during this period and has fallen off since the ban. However, the lack of research data means it is unclear how changes

---

96 www.talktofrank.com (accessed July 09).

97 The ban was precipitated by the political and media storm that blew up around smart shop sales following a series of incidents (all involving tourists) prominently including the death of a young French tourist who had allegedly taken magic mushrooms; see: www.time.com/time/world/article/0,8599,1650873,00.

98 The UK equivalent of Dutch 'smart shops', supplying 'legal highs', drug paraphernalia (pipes, bongs etc.) and drug culture books, posters and other merchandise.

99 *'How to deal with psilocybe mushrooms'*, Transform Drug Policy Foundation briefing, 2004.

in mushroom use impacted on use of other psychedelics or other more risky drugs.[100] Comparisons to other countries that did not have legal availability are hampered by poor data quality. In general, however, magic mushrooms use seems to have been generally increasing across Europe since the late 1990s, whilst LSD use has remained stable or fallen—arguably reflecting a rational consumer choice towards the less potent, shorter acting product. Lifetime use measures in the Netherlands and UK are relatively high, but last year and last month use in these countries are nearer European averages. There are other countries that have equivalent or higher levels of use, depending on which measures are used.[101] Interestingly, the 2003 ESPAD schools survey[102] found no obvious correlation between reported ease of availability and legal regimes, with the Netherlands scoring lower than the Czech Republic, Ireland, Italy, Poland and the United Kingdom for reported *'easy access'*. It seems clear that increased availability and unregulated marketing had an impact on levels of use, but, as ever, the picture is complicated by various parallel social trends.

Whilst the lack of regulation in both UK and Dutch scenarios was clearly inadequate, the availability of the mushrooms was not linked to a crisis in public health or social disorder, despite shock headlines relating to often misrepresented and isolated incidents. Given this, psilocybin mushrooms could be made legally available in a more appropriately regulated fashion with lessons learnt from previous mistakes. At a minimum, they should be sold from licensed vendors, subject to age access, packaging and labelling controls, and with strict advertising and marketing controls. These should be combined with effective targeted risk reduction information. Were this to be the case, it seems likely that psilocybin mushrooms, arguably the lowest risk psychedelic product, would cater for the vast majority of demand for psychedelics.

100 Fly-agaric mushrooms (containing the deliriant hallucinogenic compound muscimol), which are substantially more toxic than psilocybin mushrooms, have not been prohibited in the UK and remain on sale in many of the same outlets that previously sold psilocybin mushrooms.

101 See: *'Hallucinogenic mushrooms; an emerging case study'*, EMCDDA, 2006.

102 The European School Survey Project on Alcohol and Other Drugs: www.espad.org/espad-reports.

They would have additional potential for producing a substitute effect, moving recreational users away from more risky party drugs, such as stimulants and alcohol.

Further reading

* *'Hallucinogenic mushrooms; an emerging case study'*, EMCDDA, 2006
* *'How to deal with psilocybe mushrooms'*, Transform Drug Policy Foundation, 2004
* A. Weil, *'The Natural Mind: An Investigation of Drugs and the Higher Consciousness'*, Mariner Books, 1998
* P. Stafford, *'Psychedelics Encyclopaedia'*, Ronin Publishing, 1993
* *'Hallucinogenic mushrooms'*: EMCDDA drug profile
* *'LSD'*: EMCDDA drug profile

5.6   **Depressants**

Depressant drug use, including opiates, benzodiazepines, and barbiturates, is associated with a set of behaviours that are defined by a wide spectrum of motivations and functions. These range from more conventional pleasure seeking, through to relief or escape from physical or emotional pain, stress or discomfort. As such, depressant use straddles recreational and medical/quasi-medical functions, the boundaries between the two often becoming blurred. Reaching out to a population of users, a substantial fraction of whom are defined by their low levels of wellbeing, presents a unique set of policy challenges. They seek temporary solace in depressant drugs, often more as a form of functional *'self-medication'* than hedonism. Contributory factors can include emotional, psychological or mental health issues, often in combination with socio-economic deprivation.

Levels of problematic depressant use are argu-ably a closer reflection of personal and societal wellbeing than use of the other groups of drugs (for example, stimulants and psychedelics). Of course, an effective legal regulatory system should be able to dramatically reduce the harms associated with such use. However, the special qualities motivating depressant use again high-light the centrality of the wider social policy context in drug policy. In the long term, we can only reduce problematic depressant use by addressing the underlying causes of low levels of personal and social wellbeing.

Reaching out to a population of users, a substantial fraction of whom are defined by their low levels of well-being, presents a unique set of policy challenges

It is important to highlight that alcohol is also a depressant drug, even if in low to medium doses it functions as a dis-inhibitor and thus appears to have stimulant properties. Problematic alcohol consump-tion shares characteristics which parallel those of prescription and illicitly used depressants.

Two key characteristics of the depressant drug risk profile have impli-cations for depressant regulation. Firstly, whilst the chronic toxicity of depressants varies widely, they share a high overdose potential. As central nervous system depressants, the threshold at which the drugs' desired effects can become dangerous, potentially leading to uncon-sciousness, coma or death, is often relatively small. A particular risk is presented when depressant drugs are used in combination—most commonly alcohol in combination with prescription or illicit depressants. Secondly, they have a relatively high potential for dependent patterns of use to develop. Depressants can all produce potentially powerful physi-ological withdrawal effects (with barbiturates, for example, sometimes even fatal) and cravings, as well as development of tolerance. The psycho-social component of dependence can also be profound—particularly in the context of their use as self-medication, or escapism.

5.6.1 **Opiates**

An extensive group of drugs, with similar molecular structures and shared characteristics, fall within the opiates grouping.

Key amongst these are:

* **Naturally occurring opiates** in the opium poppy; morphine, codeine[103] and thebaine—in combination in the poppy resin as opium[104] or in an opium tincture with alcohol as laudanum.
* **Semi-synthetic opiates** derived from these, including oxycodone (in pharmaceutical form also under the brand name OxyContin[105]), hydrocodone (under the brandname of Dicodid, or more commonly, combined with paracetamol, as Vicodin[106]) and diamorphine, also known as heroin—its original pharmaceutical brand name, that has effectively become its generic title.
* **Fully-synthetic opiates**—including methadone, pethadine, fentanyl and tramadol.

Patterns of opiate use vary greatly between countries and regions. These reflect the varied histories of availability of the range of opiates over the past two centuries, localised opiate cultures that have formed around this availability, and the wider social, economic and cultural contexts alluded to above. Trying to devise effective policy responses to the issues around opiate use requires the grouping being viewed as a whole; there is clearly a high degree of displacement possible between opiates with similar effects, or different preparations and methods of using the same opiates. To a lesser extent other depressant drugs, and drug use more broadly, should be considered in this context.

103 Codeine is available in various over the counter pain relief products, usually in combination with paracetamol e.g. Solpadeine.

104 Opium also contains a number of other active drugs at lower levels.

105 OxyContin is one of a number of branded and generic oxycodone pharmaceutical preparations that also includes preparations with paracetamol (acetaminophen also known in branded form as Percocet), aspirin (branded form Percodan), and Ibuprofen (branded form Combunox).

106 Vicodin is one of many branded and generic pharmaceutical hydrocodone preparations used in pain relief, that also includes Lortab (with aspirin), and Vicoprofen (with ibuprofen).

Policy responses to opiates have to balance the short term goal of reducing harms associated with opiate use as it exists now—particularly the disproportionate harms generated by injected use—with the longer term goal of broader reduction of problematic opiate use and opiate related harms. Short and long term efforts should work together to help shift use from more to less risky products (both drug and preparation), using environments, and using behaviours. Taken together, they should reduce opiate dependency, and achieve longer term reductions in demand by removing obstacles to addressing the wider social policy concerns that underlie problematic use of opiates and other drugs.

Safer environments: Vancouver's Insite supervised injecting venue (above), and an open air drug scene in the back alley immediately opposite

The crossover between extensive formal use of medical opiates, and informal quasi-medical and recreational use, presents a particular set of challenges. As mentioned in *chapter 2* (and *Appendix 2*), almost half of global opium production is for legal medical pharmaceutical production. Particular care must be taken to avoid a key current problem; fear of encouraging illicit or non-medical recreational use of opiates has often restricted access for essential medical purposes, including palliative care and wider pain relief.

As alluded to in *chapter 2*, pragmatic approaches will start with an exploration of the potential for creating a clear harm reduction gradient. This will demand the differential application of regulation, along key risk vectors. It is proposed this could involve a tiered regulatory system:

❖ Some highly potent, short-acting synthetic or semi-synthetic opiates, such as fentanyl (and its various analogues), would remain prohibited under all circumstances for non-medical supply and use. Whilst many of these drugs have occasionally appeared within opiate using populations (usually as diverted medical supplies) such use is primarily a reflection of the lack of access to alternatives. If greater access to and choice of other opiates were available, it is assumed that the demand for more niche medical opiates would largely disappear.

* Where regulated access is permitted, the most severe restrictions would be applied to injectable opiates, predominantly diamorphine/heroin, which present the greatest risk. These would be available on a medical prescription basis, where specific criteria were met. Opiate prescribing models have a long history in a number of countries and are well established. As discussed in *chapter 2*, various models exist that can include access that is conditional on supervised use in a clinical setting.

* A range of oral pill or solution form pharmaceutical opiates would be available under a licensed pharmacy vendor/licensed user model. These would potentially be in combination with licensed premises for supply and consumption, or membership based clubs/venues. Specific levels of regulation for particular products would be determined by risk assessment of individual preparations. These would be combined with an assessment of local demand, patterns of use and risk behaviours. The emphasis would be on lower dose, slower release oral preparations. Some more potent/risky products would not be available, and would remain restricted for medical use only. Some non-injectable pharmaceutical opiates (including methadone) would also be available on prescription under certain circumstances. These could be subject to tighter restrictions including, for example, a requirement for supervised consumption.

*   Unrefined or moderately refined opium would be subject to relatively less restrictive controls—it would be available for smoking or oral consumption (including as poppy tea), under a licensed vendor/premises/user model, a licensed user/pharmacy sales model, or in some circumstances, on prescription. The aim of making opium subject to less restrictive availability controls, would be to reverse the trend towards more concentrated opiate products that has unfolded over the last century of prohibition. Lower risk opium preparations could absorb an increasingly large share of the demand for opiates currently met from illicit sales and diverted medical supplies of higher risk opiates. Availability for consumption in regulated venues would allow for a range of controls, peer support, risk reduction and targeting of public health information and services.

Appendices

Appendix 1:

Reforming the UN drug control system

The problem: lack of flexibility

Attempts to move along the spectrum of available drug policy options, away from punitive prohibitionist approaches towards decriminalisation of adult use and, more specifically, legal regulation of drug production and supply for non medical use, inevitably run into the legal and institutional obstacles created by the three UN drug conventions (1961, 1971, and 1988—detailed below).

It is notable that whilst the conventions draw very strict lines in terms of movement in one direction along the policy continuum, few barriers or parameters exist for movement in the opposite direction, towards increasing strictness, although the 1988 convention notes that this is *'subject always'* to human rights law. The International Narcotics Control Board (INCB—see below) has rarely publicly spoken out against excessively punitive responses to drug use[107] even when these have involved serious human rights violations; for example, the use of the death penalty for drug offences (in direct violation of international law[108] and the UN General Assembly[109]), and the extrajudicial execution of over 2000 citizens during the War on Drugs crackdown in Thailand in 2003.

This is in stark contrast to its frequent and vocal protestations at even the most minor shifts in the opposite direction. It is only in the very recent history of the UN drug machinery, following a concerted effort from various civil society groups and NGOs, that human rights have featured in Commission on Narcotic Drugs (CND) and UN Office on Drugs and Crime (UNODC) deliberations in any meaningful way.[110]

The challenge: allowing increased flexibility without undermining the whole system.

The challenge in reforming the international drug control infrastructure is to institute reforms that remove the barriers to individual or groups of states exploring models for the legal regulation and supply of some currently illicit drugs, without destroying the entire international drug control infrastructure, much of which is unquestionably beneficial. The system of control and regulation of the pharmaceutical trade is vitally important. The consensus and shared purpose that the conventions represent—behind the need to address the problems associated with drugs—holds great potential to develop and implement more effective responses at an international level, guided by the principles and norms of the United Nations.

Background to the UN conventions

The present system of worldwide drug control is regulated by three international conventions. These are the 1961 Single Convention on Narcotic Drugs, as amended by the 1972 Protocol, the 1971 Convention on Psychotropic Substances and the 1988 Convention against Illicit

---

108 R. Lines, '*The Death Penalty for Drug Offences*', HR2, IHRA, 2008.

109 The UN General Assembly adopted a resolution calling for a moratorium on the use of the death penalty in 2007. See: www.un.org/News/Press/docs/2007/ga10678.doc.

110 D. Barrett, '*Recalibrating the Regime*', IHRA, Human Rights Watch, CHALN, 2008.

Traffic in Narcotic Drugs and Psychotropic Substances.[111] As of March 2008, 183 states are parties to all three conventions.

The 1961 Convention on Narcotic Drugs

The bedrock of the global drug control regime is the 1961 Single Convention, so called because it largely replaced the previous international agreements that had been developing piecemeal since the early years of the twentieth century. Arguably the first and most significant of these was the Hague Opium Convention of 1912, that resulted from the Shanghai Opium Commission organised by the US in 1909. The thirteen countries involved all sought to curb the opium trade (albeit for a range of different cultural, geo-political and economic reasons). The Hague convention that emerged in 1912 established the model for international drug control that continues to this day, binding parties to limit production, supply and use of opium to medical contexts, coordinate international efforts to enforce restrictions on non-medical use including closure of *'opium dens'*, and specifically to penalise unauthorised possession. It is interesting to note that drug control demonstrates a reversed evolutionary pattern of development to much of contemporary social, criminal or public health policy, in that it actually began with a top-down international approach that was then consolidated into domestic policy and law at a later stage.[112]

The 1961 Convention outlines the same prohibitionist principles as its forerunner, but for a far broader spectrum of drugs, and also involving a substantially greater number of state parties. It shaped global and domestic drug policy for the next half century. In a similar fashion to the Hague opium convention, the 1961 convention, as a general obligation,

'...we believe the time has come for the international treaties to be reconsidered' and recommended that '...the Government initiates a discussion within the Commission on Narcotic Drugs of alternative ways— including the possibility of legalisation and regulation—to tackle the global drugs dilemma.'

The UK House of Commons Home Affairs Select Committee 2001 report *'The Government's Drugs Policy: Is It Working?'*

---

111 All three treaties available in full from the UNODC website: www.unodc.org.

112 A. Jamieson, *'International drug conventions, national compliance and the UN commentaries: the shaming mechanism'*, in N. Dorn, A. Jamieson, *'European Drug Laws: the Room for Manœuvre'*, Drugscope, 2001.

under Article 4(c) requires signatory nations to limit the production, manufacture, export, import, distribution of, trade in, use and possession of named drugs exclusively to *'medical and scientific purposes'*.

Reflecting the prevalent concerns of the era (bearing in mind that the main text of the convention was drafted in the 1950s, some of it as far back as the 1940s[113]), the Convention pays particular attention to plant based drugs: opium, coca, and cannabis (along with derived drugs heroin and cocaine). In fact more than one hundred illicit substances are placed in four schedules, nominally based on the perceived harmfulness (specifically addictiveness) of the drug as was understood at the time.[114] Notably the Universal Declaration of Human Rights drafting period (1946–48) overlapped the Single Convention drafting to some extent, and had been in place for thirteen years by its enactment. It does not appear to have influenced the Single Convention's negotiations, the absence of any reference to the Universal Declaration in the Single Convention's preamble being particularly conspicuous.

Article 2 of the Single Convention determines that the supply or dispensing of any scheduled substance is only possible under legal authority, namely under licence.

* Schedule I contains substances that are subject to all of the control measures under the Convention, including heroin, cocaine and cannabis.
* Schedule II is comprised of substances used for medical purposes that are deemed to require less stringent control in view of a lesser risk of abuse, such as codeine.
* Schedule III is effectively for exemptions and, as such, excludes a series of pharmaceutical preparations made from substances perceived not to lead to abuse or ill effects, such as powders and liquids with very low dosages of opium or cocaine.

---

113 To put this in perspective, Al Capone died in 1947.

114 How these rankings were determined remains murky and there has been a growing body of critique about anomalies in the rankings and the broader utility of a scheduling system (see: chapter 4.2, page 70).

✻ Schedule IV substances are permitted for amounts that may be necessary for medical and scientific research. This includes some substances from Schedule I, when they are considered to have particularly dangerous properties which are not offset by therapeutic value that cannot be afforded by some other drug.

The Single Convention also established the International Narcotics Control Board (INCB) within the UN international drug control system. It is the self-described *'independent and quasi-judicial monitoring body for the implementation of the United Nations international drug control conventions'.*[115] The INCB has a watchdog role over the conventions, in theory much like similar agencies that exist to monitor compliance to other UN treaties[116]. However, criticisms of the INCB's activities have been growing. It has increasingly been seen as inflexible and uncompromising, acting as *'guardian'* of the purity of the conventions— challenging activity that does not fit with its rigid interpretations of the treaty—and non-responsive to the needs of member states in a world dramatically changed from that in which the INCB was established (see: *Further reading*, below).

The 1971 Convention on Psychotropic Substances

The 1971 convention was constructed as a response to concern about emerging drugs and related behaviours during the 1960s, specifically the higher profile synthetic and/or prescribable drugs,[117] including amphetamine-like stimulants, barbiturates and other sedative-hypnotics/depressants, and hallucinogens (most notoriously, at this point, LSD). These are similarly classified into four schedules according to perceived harm and therapeutic value, with a corresponding hierarchy

---

115 See: INCB, *'Mandate and Functions'*, www.incb.org/incb/mandate.

116 The ultimate arbiter between parties regarding disputes over the conventions is the International Court of Justice.

117 The UN drug agencies label such synthetic drugs *'psychotropic substances'*—hence the name of the 1971 convention, as distinct from the 'narcotic drugs', the plant based drugs that are the primary concern of the 1961 convention. The use of the term *'narcotic'* is rather confusing given its historical meaning as inducing sleep or numbness. Despite the term being rather outdated and redundant, in the US and UN legal context 'narcotic' has increasingly been used to describe any illegal drug rather than a drug with a given effect.

of controls to license medical, scientific,
or other uses.

An important purpose of both the 1961
and 1971 Conventions was to codify internationally appropriate control measures
to ensure the availability of drugs for
medical and scientific purposes, while
preventing leakage into illicit channels.
It is in this context that the World Health
Organization (WHO) is responsible for
the medical and scientific assessment of
all psychoactive substances, and subsequent advice to the Commission on
Narcotic Drugs (CND or Commission)
about the classification of drugs into one of the schedules of the 1961
and 1971 treaties (including changes to classifications).

1988 Convention against Illicit Traffic in Narcotic Drugs and Psychotropic Substances

The 1988 Convention was primarily designed to deal with the growth of
international trafficking in illegal substances in the 1970s and 1980s. The
earlier international instruments had failed to achieve the aspiration of
preventing the production, trafficking and supply of scheduled drugs in
quite spectacular style. The 1988 convention can be seen as a response
to this failure and the perceived inadequacies of earlier treaties in this
regard. As such it provides a raft of measures against drug trafficking
and precursor chemicals. The INCB website notes that it:

> ...provides comprehensive measures against drug trafficking, including
> provisions against money laundering and the diversion of precursor
> chemicals. It provides for international cooperation through, for

example, extradition of drug traffickers, controlled deliveries and transfer of proceedings.

Within the treaty the precursor chemicals are themselves scheduled in a similar fashion to the drugs covered by the previous treaties.

Unlike the 1961 and 1971 conventions, which focused almost exclusively on drug production and supply issues, the 1988 Convention made a significant departure by also incorporating drug demand within one key paragraph (paragraph 2 of Article 3) which directly concerns criminalisation of drug users. It states unequivocally that:

> *...each Party shall adopt such measures as may be necessary to establish as a criminal offence under its domestic law, when committed intentionally, the possession, purchase or cultivation of narcotic drugs or psychotropic substances for personal consumption contrary to the provisions of the 1961 Convention, the 1961 Convention as amended or the 1971 Convention.*[118]

This is far more specific than the previous conventions' vague calls for criminalisation of possession. As the commentary on the 1988 convention says explicitly, this paragraph *'amounts in fact also to a penalisation of personal consumption'.*[119] There are few comparable UN conventions that specifically prescribe criminal penalties for individual adult conduct, as opposed to the state or government actions on which most conventions are focused.

The only even vaguely comparable convention-based prohibitions against individual actions are for torture, crimes against humanity including genocide, acts of terrorism, human trafficking and sexual

---

118 Notably this paragraph is introduced with the caveat that it is, 'Subject to its constitutional principles and the basic concepts of its legal system'.

119 *'Commentary on the United Nations Convention Against Illicit Traffic in Narcotic Drugs and Psychotropic Substances'*, New York, United Nations Publications, E/CN.7/590, December, 1988. Such commentaries are official (non-binding) UN discursive documents produced retrospectively to provide legal guidance on the interpretation and implementation of the conventions.

exploitation of children. These are evidently of a different order of magnitude to consenting adult drug use.

A crisis within the system

The crisis within the UN drug control system that is driving the reform debate has a number of facets:

* **Long term systemic failure on its own terms**: the UN drug agencies' self-proclaimed goal of *'a drug free world'* is, by its own admission, further away than ever. UNODC rhetoric now talks more about *'containment'* than *'eradication'*, but even this position is unsustainable in light of deteriorating outcomes on almost all meaningful measures.

* **Challenges, tensions and contradictions created by harm reduction:** whilst the harm reduction movement (as distinct from the legalisation/regulation movement) largely seeks reforms within the existing legal framework, it none the less represents a series of profound contradictions for UN global drug control infrastructure. The tenets of harm reduction are

UN Commission on Narcotic Drugs, Vienna, 2008

STEPHEN ROLLES

often fundamentally at odds with those that underlie prohibition and that shaped the treaties during the last century. It is also impossible to ignore the fact that much of the harm that the movement seeks to reduce directly or indirectly results from prohibition and its enforcement (see: *4.2 Assessing and ranking drug harms*, page 70). These tensions are being played out between the UN drug entities (particularly the CND and INCB) and other members of the UN family (notably the UNAIDS, the WHO) and between increasingly polarised groupings of reform and prohibition oriented member states.

✢ **Challenges posed by decriminalisation**: The growing global trend towards actual or *de facto* decriminalisation of personal possession/use of drugs, whilst nominally permitted within the treaties, like harm reduction, poses serious practical and intellectual challenges to the status quo in the longer term. Such reforms not only challenge the spirit of the conventions but are now pushing the *'room to manœuvre'* to its limits, and arguably beyond.

Flexibility in the conventions?

It is important to appreciate that none of the conventions are *'self-executing'*. That is, while the conventions impose obligations on states to apply international law, such law is not directly or immediately enforceable. This contrasts with, for example, the European Convention on Human Rights status in the UK, where it has been incorporated into domestic law. The conventions effectively remain contracts between states. This contractual nature, bolstered by a large number of signatories, is arguably the real source of their power.

The INCB, as the body responsible for overseeing the operation of the treaties, has no formal power to enforce the implementation of the conventions' various provisions or punish for non compliance. However, considerable public opprobrium can follow its often vocal criticism of individual state actions, usually made in its annual report.[120]

Obviously states are required to interpret and implement UN treaties in good faith, respecting the *'object and purpose'* of conventions to which they are party; an attitude that is required for the UN treaty system to have any coherence, stability and authority.[121] As such, and despite the fact that as already noted the autonomy of domestic law is stressed within all the conventions,[122] state parties are required, or at the very least expected to adhere to, the standards and norms of the global drug control systems.

However, the system and wording of the international conventions certainly leaves considerable room for interpretation at the national level. They offer signatory nations more *'room for manœuvre'* in formulating and implementing domestic policy and enforcement strategies than is often appreciated in popular political and media discourse. This explains why, despite the apparent consensus behind the conventions, there are wide variations in the way they are interpreted and implemented. Many of these interpretations would seem to push at the boundaries of the letter and spirit of the conventions (see above).

Some, most notably the INCB, have argued that certain moves—particularly high profile reforms such as reductions in cannabis penalties or *de facto* decriminalisation of cannabis, and harm reduction interventions including supervised injecting rooms (and until recently even needle exchange[123])—are contrary to or go against the *'spirit of the Conventions'*, especially the stricter provisions of the 1988 Convention.

---

120 By way of contrast the European Court of Human Rights and the European Court of Justice have more direct enforcement powers regarding Council of Europe and EU treaties and directives respectively. Human Rights treaty bodies—although their main form of sanction is political—also have quasi judicial procedures that can suggest remedies including compensation.

121 This is also specifically determined by the Vienna Convention on the law of treaties, article 31 (essentially a treaty that codifies customary law on treaties as the legal basis of the convention system).

122 This is in terms of flexibility and interpretation and does not allow national law to be cited to excuse non-performance of a treaty (See article 27 of the Vienna Convention).

123 According to former INCB president Philip O. Emafo, needle exchanges should be regarded as *'contrary to the provisions of the conventions'*. Interview in *'Update'*, UNODC, December 2002.

None the less the nations in question have a strong legal position when contending that they are still operating inside the parameters of the international legislation.[124]

Additional latitude is also provided by the fact that the Single Convention does not define *'medical and scientific purposes'*. For practical reasons the framers of the 1961 Convention could not be over-prescriptive with such terms, tacitly acknowledging that they would inevitably have different meanings in different countries and cultures and will doubtless also shift and change in time. Many harm reduction initiatives that remain controversial with the INCB in particular, are legitimately argued to be medical interventions—prevention of HIV being the most obvious and politically potent.

Thus, when adopting the limited reforms that have so far taken place, such as needle exchange and supervised injecting, individual states have not incurred sufficient international political repercussions to force them to forgo the benefits of those policies. Moreover, defence of such reforms in the UN arena has been bolstered by the fact that they have been adopted by a number of countries, and have been subject to unprecedented scrutiny. In fact, many are now supported by a substantial body of evidence, showing that when done properly, they can deliver positive public health and criminal justice outcomes.[125] This *'strength in numbers'* defensive position points to potential ways forward for certain future reforms, as discussed below.

Despite this controversial grey area at the fringes of what is permitted within the conventions, there can be no doubt that they are very specifically prohibitionist in nature. In their current form, they offer no room for any substantial form of legally regulated production, supply or use for non medical use, beyond the small amount of crossover that

124 For example; methadone treatment is specifically allowed under the conventions as noted in the 1988 commentary, and in 2002 the INCB itself commissioned a legal opinion on supervised injecting rooms from the UNDCP Legal Affairs Section; titled *'Flexibility of Treaty Provisions as regards Harm Reduction Approaches'*, which concluded that substitution treatment, needle exchanges and supervised injecting rooms do not breach the conventions.

125 For example: Insite, Vancouver's supervised injecting facility.

inevitably occurs with some of the medical access models currently in place. In any case, these existing models focus on a minority of problematic users rather than the majority of non problematic users. Flexibility that may be potentially available regarding lenience towards drug users, according to objective interpretations of the law, is simply not present when it comes to options regarding legal regulation of drug production and supply for non medical use. Bewley-Taylor (2005) notes that:

Nations may currently be pushing the boundaries of the international system, but the pursuit of any action to formally legalise non-medical and scientific drug use would require either treaty revision or a complete or partial withdrawal from the current regime.

Options for reforming the UN drug control system:

Treaty revision

The 1997 UN World Drugs Report, produced by the UN Drug Control Program[126] notes that:

Laws—and even the International Conventions—are not written in stone; they can be changed when the democratic will of nations so wishes it.[127]

There are clearly expressed mechanisms in the drug conventions (as with all conventions) for them to be revised. Two possible routes exist in this respect: modification and amendment. Bewley-Taylor[128] summarises these options thus:

Modification refers to a possible alteration in the regime through the re-scheduling of a drug, that is to say moving it from one to another

---

126 Later absorbed within the current UN Office on Drugs and Crime (UNODC).

127 UNODC World Drug Report 1997, chapter 8: *'The Regulation-Legalization Debate'*. The next sentence (the final one of the chapter as it happens) is: 'But the legalizers must find better answers to the trickier questions before hearts and minds across the world will follow them'.

128 D. Bewley-Taylor, *'Challenging the UN drug control conventions: problems and possibilities'*, International Journal of Drug Policy, 2003, Vol. 14, pages 171–179.

of the 1961 and 1971 Convention schedules or the 1988 Convention
tables, or through the deletion of a drug from a schedule/schedules
or table/tables altogether. Amendment refers to the formal altera-
tion of treaty provisions, namely a convention article, which affects
all the Parties.

Bewley-Taylor is one of a number of Convention scholars to have detailed the practical difficulties in achieving much substantive reform using either of these mechanisms.

Modification

Article 3 of the Single Convention allows for the WHO or any Party state to initiate the modification process that would reschedule a specified drug or delete it from the conventions at any time. For cannabis and coca an amendment to the Single Convention would also be required as cultivation and production of the plants is specifically prohibited, separately from the scheduling infrastructure—thus drastically limiting the reform possibilities theoretically available for other scheduled drugs. The nature of the Convention provisions renders this somewhat academic, as individual states have the power within the system to easily block change. The WHO, whilst key to any modification process because of its advisory role, can only make non-binding recommendations—the power to implement changes remains with the 53 member Commission on Narcotic Drugs that operates within and determines policy for the UNODC.

Within the CND there exists a curious alliance of states (including Sweden, Japan, many ex-Soviet States, most Arab nations and the USA) that are staunchly opposed to any revisions that would move the treaty away from its punitive tenets. For these countries the conventions are based on the rigid and absolute position that *all* (illegal) drug use is morally unacceptable—to the extent that the conventions have assumed a status more akin to religious documents.[129] In effect, unlike the statement in the 1997

129 P. Cohen, *'The drug prohibition church and the adventure of reformation'*, International
Journal of Drug Policy, 2003, Vol. 14:2, pages 213–215.

177

UN world drugs report (*above*), for these countries the conventions are, to all intents and purposes, indeed written in stone.

The mechanisms for change within all three conventions provide this group with ample opportunity to stifle any revisionist action. Within this significant power block the US unsurprisingly plays the central hegemonic role. The US was the driving force behind the conventions in the first instance (their prohibitionist nature mirroring the US's historic cultural tendencies) and has, through its support for them and indeed through other forms of political pressure (including its certification system) been their significant bulwark. As a diplomat at the UN in Vienna observed only a few years ago, '*wherever a nation seems about to break ranks [with Washington's views on prohibition] the US will be there, cajoling or threatening*'.[130]

The make-up of the Commission means that consensus on revisionist moves would never be established. Even in the event of a move to a vote, which the political culture in Vienna renders highly unlikely, the majority would be unlikely to be established. Even if accepted by the CND, any state can request the modification be referred to the UN Economic and Social Council (ECOSOC), whose decision is final; the same hurdles with the prohibitionist states would be faced again.

Similar structures, with minor administrative variations, exist for the 1971 and 1988 conventions (1971 requires a two thirds rather than simple majority decision from CND).

Amendment

The obstacles to modification render it an effectively worthless option, making the prospects for amendment seem initially more promising. However, once again there is ample scope for opposing parties to block changes.

130 Webster, 1998, quoted in D. Bewley-Taylor, '*Emerging policy contradictions between the United Nations drug control system and the core values of the United Nations*', International Journal of Drug Policy, 2005, Vol. 16, pages 423–431.

The possibility to amend is provided in Article 47 of the Single Convention, Article 30 of the 1971 Convention and Article 31 of the 1988 Convention. Parties can notify the Secretary-General of a proposed amendment, including the reasoning behind the move. The Secretary-General then communicates the proposed amendment and the reasons for it to the Parties and to the Council. It is then the ECOSOC's decision to either call a conference to consider the amendment, or ask the parties if they accept the amendment. In the unlikely event of no party rejecting the amendment within 18 months the amendment comes into force.

In the more likely event of objections being raised to ECOSOC, the council then can decide whether or not to convene a conference to consider the amendment. Such a conference could usefully raise the profile of the revision issue, but there would be no guarantee of meaningful revisions. Prohibition oriented states could even potentially exploit the event to move policy in the opposite direction.[131] Functional cost objections could also be made to such a conference—that is, that it would be too expensive.

Other revision options

Although not outlined in the relevant articles of the conventions there are additional routes by which amendments may be put forward. For example, according to the Commentary on the Single Convention, ECOSOC may submit proposed amendments to the General Assembly for consideration in accordance with Article 62 paragraph 3 of the UN Charter. The General Assembly may itself also take the initiative in amending the Convention, either by adopting revisions, or by calling a Plenipotentiary Conference for this purpose. The same goes for the 1971 and 1988 Conventions.

Nonetheless, considering the complex political dynamics of the General Assembly, there is no reason to suggest that such alternative

---

131 This occurred during and after behind the scenes activity in the run up to the 1998 United Nations General Assembly Special Session on Drugs (UNGASS). Then initial efforts to reassess the effectiveness of the drug control regime were reduced to a reaffirmation of the current system and its strategies.

amendment procedures would circumvent the obstacles presented by the prohibition-oriented block when following the rules laid out in the specific articles.

In order to cut this particular Gordian knot, parties may wish to consider withdrawing from the treaties.

Withdrawal from the treaties

The administrative blocking possibilities within the convention review procedures mean that the prohibitionist block can effectively ensure no undesirable revisions are made. The only option then available to an individual state wishing to operate outside of the conventions would be to withdraw from the relevant treaty. Two main options exist for such a withdrawal from the drugs treaties; while in the context of international relations and UN culture they would be seen as extreme, they would remain within the confines of international law, as they are technically allowed by articles of the treaties.

The possibilities of denunciation

Articles within all the treaties allow any Party to opt out by depositing a denunciation with the Secretary-General in writing, and including reference to the legal grounds for the move. With regard to the 1961 and 1971 Conventions, if the Secretary-General receives this instrument on or before the first of July, the denunciation comes into effect for that Party at the beginning of the following year. Denunciation of the 1988 Convention comes into effect for the denouncing Party one year after the receipt of the notification by the Secretary-General.

As of March 2008 it would, however, require 143 individual state denunciations to reduce the number of ratifications of the 1961 Convention to below 40, thus triggering its termination (in accordance with Article 41).

'Looking back over the last century, we can see that the control system and its application have had several unintended consequences — they may or may not have been unexpected but they were certainly unintended.

'The first unintended consequence is a huge criminal black market that thrives in order to get prohibited substances from producers to consumers, whether driven by a 'supply push' or a 'demand pull', the financial incentives to enter this market are enormous. There is no shortage of criminals competing to claw out a share of a market in which hundred fold increases in price from production to retail are not uncommon.

'The second unintended consequence is what one night call policy displacement. Public health, which is clearly the first principle of drug control... was displaced into the background.

'The third unintended consequence is geographical displacement. It is often called the balloon effect because squeezing (by tighter controls) one place produces a swelling (namely an increase) in another place...'

Antonio Maria Costa, Executive Director of UN Office on Drugs and Crime, *'Making drug control "fit for purpose": Building on the UNGASS decade'*, page 10

It needs to be acknowledged that this is incredibly unlikely, even if theoretically possible or even desirable. The 1988 Convention in fact has no termination clause and would thus, in accordance with Article 55 of the Vienna Convention on the Law of Treaties, somewhat bizarrely remain in force even if there was only one remaining signatory.

It should also be clearly acknowledged that, beyond the possibilities of what is technically allowed, the political consequences for any individual state that opted out of the prohibitionist regime in this way could potentially be severe. Criticism from the prohibitionist block would be a serious impediment, particularly from the US, UNODC and the INCB.

US scholar Peter Andreas notes that:

Open defection from the drug prohibition regime would... have severe consequences: it would place the defecting country in the category of a pariah 'narco-state', generate material repercussions in the form of

economic sanctions and aid cut-offs, and damage the country's moral
standing in the international community.[132]

Developed countries would obviously be better positioned to resist pressure from the US, as would states less dependent on US trade or aid. The Netherlands for example has taken criticism for years because of its coffee shop cannabis system, but even they have not opted out of the treaties, instead choosing to operate at the fringes of what is allowable in their letter and spirit.

Whilst an individual state may choose to opt out in certain circumstances it seems highly unlikely, although not unheard of; between 1945 and 2004 there were 1547 denunciations of withdrawals from UN treaties—just under 5% of the total number of ratifications[133] (none of these addressed the drug treaties). Far more likely is that a group of like-minded revision oriented states would collectively mount a challenge to the system. Bewley-Taylor[134] suggests that:

> *If a credible group of Parties from Europe, Australasia and the Group*
> *of Latin American and Caribbean countries at the UN (the so-called*
> *GRULAC), for example, were to combine to denounce one or all of the*
> *treaties, the US-UN axis may lose much of its potential influence. The*
> *'denouncers' may find safety in numbers and quite legitimately walk*
> *away from the treaties.*

Bewley-Taylor also suggests that even the threat of such action could be enough to precipitate substantial reform, allowing the system to be revised in such a way as to facilitate far more flexibility along the spectrum of policy options than the existing barriers created by the absolutist prohibitionist structures currently permit. The prohibitionist states could give way to partial reforms, if they were placed in

---

132 Quoted in Bewley-Taylor, 2003.

133 L. Helfer, *'Exiting treaties'*, 2005, Virginia Law Review 91: 1579–1648.

134 D. Bewley-Taylor, *'Emerging policy contradictions between the United Nations drug control system and the core values of the United Nations'*, International Journal of Drug Policy, 2005, Vol.16.6, pages 423–431.

a situation where any refusal to do so threatened the entire drug treaty system. Bewley-Taylor notes that:

> *Such a scenario is possible since it is generally agreed that denunciation of any treaty can lead to its demise. This would likely be the case with regard to any of the drug control treaties due to the nature of the issue and the convention's reliance on widespread transnational adherence. Using denunciation as a trigger for treaty revision would differ from the procedures to modify the conventions discussed above since a group of like minded states would not simply be playing the numbers game in an effort to gain majority decisions in both the Council or the Commission. A sufficiently weighty 'denouncers' group may be able to not only withstand UN-US pressure, but also apply significant pressure itself.*

The Beckley Foundation's Global Cannabis commission report identifies an additional possibility,[135] arguably more attractive from a political perspective, of denunciation followed by re-accession with a reservation. The commission highlights the technical problems with this course of action but does note that both the Netherlands and Switzerland made reservations against the application of some of the provisions on criminalisation (in Article 3) when they ratified the 1988 Convention.

Other possibilities for treaty reform

The United Nations Drug Control Programme (UNDCP) 1997 World Drug Report states:

> *. . . [none of the] three international drug Conventions insist on the establishment of drug consumption per se as a punishable offence. Only the 1988 Convention clearly requires parties to establish as criminal offences under law the possession, purchase or cultivation of*

135 Beckley Foundation, '*Global Cannabis Commission*', 2008, page 155 (note: the discussion is limited to cannabis rather than the more substantive debate around all options for all currently illegal drugs).

controlled drugs for the purpose of non-medical, personal consump-
tion, unless to do so would be contrary to the constitutional principles
and basic concepts of their legal systems.

As has already been alluded to, if the constitutional courts in a signatory nation determined and ruled prohibition of a single drug, group of,
or even all drugs, was contrary to their constitutional principles then
the party would effectively be no longer bound by the limitations of
the Conventions with respect to those drugs. An active debate already
exists with regard to the possibilities of challenging drug prohibition
on the grounds of human rights violations, that might allow some way
to exploit this constitutional principles *'loophole'*.

Once again, pursuing this course of action would incur the wrath of the
prohibitionist block and their strategic/ideological allies in drug control
thinking, and not be without political consequences. But similarly a
group of reform oriented nations acting together could find strength in
numbers to withstand any ensuing pressure. Such a defection would, as
Bewley-Taylor describes it, *'severely weaken the treaty system and possibly*
act as a trigger for regime change'.

Two further technical possibilities exist. One would be if a new treaty
were drafted and adopted on the same subject, superseding the previous
treaties and those bound by them. A second would be if, for example,
something such as the right of indigenous people to sovereignty over
natural resources were to become recognised as *jus cogens* (i.e. a peremp-
tory norm of international law), then anything in conflict with it would
become null and void. Both of these possibilities are constrained by the
political impediments outlined above.

Disregarding the treaties

Parties could simply ignore all or part of the treaties. If multiple states engaged in such a strategy, the treaties would eventually *'wither on the vine'*, falling into disuse without any specific termination or reform. An individual country disregarding the treaties, or applying them only partially, could in this way institute any policies deemed to be necessary at the national level, including arguably the most likely example: the actual legalisation of cannabis and the introduction of a licensing system for domestic producers (as the Netherlands and Switzerland have been debating at the parliamentary level for some years, and which is now on the political agenda in a number of US states).

'I say drug use cannot be criminalised. I'm talking about criminalising trafficking but not users. From a scientific perspective, I cannot understand the repressive policy perspective.'

Michele Kazatchkine, Head of the Global Fund to fight AIDS, TB and Malaria[136]

Such a move however, like all the other possible reforms discussed here, raises serious issues that go beyond the realm of drug control—particularly if taken unilaterally. The possibility of nations unilaterally ignoring drug control treaty commitments could threaten, or be perceived to threaten, the stability of the entire treaty system. The cost of such a threat and the benefits derived from the wider UN treaty system would make states wary of opting out, even on a limited reform such as cannabis production.

As determined by the Vienna Convention on the Law of Treaties 1969, article 62, all treaties can naturally cease to be binding when a fundamental change of circumstances has occurred since the time of signing. This could be argued with regard to the fundamental change in the nature and scope of the international drug phenomenon that has taken place since 1961, meaning this doctrine of *rebus sic stantibus* could potentially be applied to the drug treaties.

But, yet again, the selective application of such a principle would potentially call into question the wider validity of the many and varied conventions. The cost benefit analysis for any individual state would

---

'I look to Asian Governments to amend outdated laws criminalizing the most vulnerable sections of society, and take all the measures needed to ensure they live in dignity.

'We need to review legislation that risks hampering universal access—in cases where vulnerable groups are criminalized for their lifestyles"

UN Secretary-General Ban Ki-Moon[137]

presumably prevent action. This has not, however, prevented the US from acting in such a way with regards to its withdrawal from the Kyoto treaty (never ratified), its repudiation of the 1972 Anti-Ballistic Missile treaty (on the grounds that it was a *'relic'* of the cold war no longer relevant to the modern world), and the recent decision to un-sign itself from the Rome Statute of the International Criminal Court.

All of these actions can be seen as not only undermining the treaties themselves, but additionally threatening the wider treaty system. Indeed, the US has begun to slowly move away from some of the Bush-era decisions, as the political ramifications of those decisions have become apparent. By Bewley-Taylor's analysis:

> *In facilitating this unprecedented move the administration of George W. Bush seems to have asserted that the US is also no longer bound by the Vienna Convention on the Law of Treaties. Under the 1969 Convention, a country that has signed a treaty cannot act to defeat the purpose of that treaty, even if it does not intend to ratify it. Thus, having set this precedent on the basis of national interest, Washington will surely find itself in an awkward position vis-à-vis its opposition to any defection from the drug control treaties on similar grounds.*

Pragmatic and practical ways forward

Given the near impossibility for substantial or meaningful reform to be achieved by unilateral action, using the established administrative routes outlined in the various articles of the drug treaties and related UN legal structures, the most credible and likely way that the current treaty restrictions on exploring legal regulatory models for certain substances

137 Comments by the UN Secretary-General in relation to the report by the Independent Commission on AIDS in Asia (established by UNAIDS) is entitled *'Redefining AIDS in Asia: Crafting an Effective Response'*, March 2008.

will be loosened is clearly through some form of collective action, by a coalition of reform minded states. This coalition would likely consist predominantly of an EU bloc (presumably minus Sweden), a South and Central American bloc, possibly along with New Zealand, Australia, Canada, and various others.

This group of countries is already, through the widespread adoption of pragmatic harm reduction and tolerance policies, increasingly moving away from both the spirit and letter of certain crucial prohibitive aspects of the conventions as they stand. If these trends continue, as seems inevitable, a crisis point will be reached where the tensions between treaty commitments and actual policy implementation will mean a more substantial recasting of the conventions would be required for the overall system of drug controls to be preserved, including the valued and unquestioned benefits of the system for controlling licit pharmaceuticals.

Arguably this crisis point has already been reached or is fast approaching, as the tensions over the political declaration wording at the 2009 CND (specifically the inclusion of any mention of '*harm reduction*') demonstrated; key elements of the consensus behind the international drug control system as it stands are already beginning to crumble.

A stepped approach

Whilst the current system may be increasingly unstable and fragile as the tensions between the different camps grow, there is no prospect of it changing overnight. Any

'[It was] increasingly difficult to justify the continued distinction among substances solely according to their legal status and social acceptability. Insofar as nicotine-addiction, alcoholism, and the abuse of solvents and inhalants may represent greater threats to health than the abuse of some substances presently under international control, pragmatism would lead to the conclusion that pursuing disparate strategies to minimize their impact is ultimately artificial, irrational and uneconomical.'

Executive Director of the United Nations International Drug Control Programme at the Thirty-seventh Session of the Commission on Narcotic Drugs, Vienna 13 April 1994.

actual reform process will undoubtedly follow a protracted and difficult debate, and will be fraught with diplomatic wrangling—there is a need for realism about these hurdles. However, as the quotes in this appendix demonstrate, key figures and institutions in the UN system freely acknowledge the inappropriateness of criminalising drug users, the systemic failure and futility of supply side drug controls and interdiction, the dramatic negative unintended consequences of international supply side interdiction and enforcement efforts, and that the conventions are outdated and not fit for purpose. At the same time they now acknowledge the primacy of public health in drug policy, the centrality of the harm reduction approach and the fact that there is a spirit of reform in the air. In this context the possibilities for meaningful reform and evolution of the UN drug control system begin to look more hopeful.

Key steps towards reform will include:

❧   Moves must be made to establish meaningful international data collection. In particular, indicators not currently included in national questionnaires informing annual UN World Drug Reports should be added to those questionnaires. These include questions concerning the impact of drug control on human rights, conflict, crime, corruption, development and security—as well as the more familiar public health measures. Such data will facilitate evaluation of the UN drug control initiatives and global prohibition, significantly including their unintended consequences identified by the UNODC.[138] It will support a more effective critique of current successes and failings, which will help inform and guide more serious discussion of alternative approaches.

❧   System coherence issues within the UN family should be addressed—in particular regarding how the UN's international drug control infrastructure, and its enforcement, impact on

---

138 A. Costa, *'Making drug control "fit for purpose": Building on the UNGASS decade'*, UNODC, 2008.

'In line with various United Nations instruments, legislative and policy reforms necessary to meet the objective above should be pursued in areas including:

> *Criminal laws and penalties, with the objective of reducing the criminalization of non-violent drug offences and significantly reducing the use of incarceration for non-violent drug users.*

> *Drug control laws and penalties, with the objective of ensuring that these laws and their interpretation and enforcement are complementary to HIV/AIDS strategies and do not hinder HIV/AIDS prevention or access to HIV/AIDS treatment.*

> *Sentencing laws and practices, with the objective of developing alternatives to prison and non-custodial diversions for people convicted of offences related to drug use so as to significantly reduce the number of drug users sent to prison, the overall prison population, and levels of prison overcrowding.*

'HIV/AIDS Prevention, Care, Treatment and Support in Prison Settings; A Framework for an Effective National Response', UN Office on Drugs and Crime, co-published with the World Health Organization and the Joint United Nations Programme on HIV/AIDS

human rights, human development and human security: the three pillars of the UN. Addressing the most extreme manifestations of the drug war would be the natural first step, but there is an urgent need for the UN drug agencies to operate within the UN principles and norms from which they have been historically isolated.

✢ Fully investigating conflicts between human rights law and the drug conventions and applying concurrent human rights obligations to all drug control activities.[139]

✢ A progressive shift towards a greater role for other UN agencies including the WHO and UNAIDS. This would echo the trend in drug policy generally away from a criminal justice focus to a more public health focus (including the location of the drug brief in domestic government, for example Spain, moving from Home Affairs to Health). This would promote a more pragmatic and evidence-based discourse.

---

[139] For more detailed discussion see: D. Barrett, M. Novak, *'The United Nations and Drug Policy, Towards a human rights based approach'* (in: *'The diversity of international law: Essays in honour of Kalliopi K Koufa'*), 2009.

* A single heavy-weight country *'taking the plunge'*, making its position known and putting more substantive treaty system reform on the CND agenda, whilst simultaneously exercising leadership in building a coalition of reform states. The group of twenty six states that emerged during the 2009 High Level Segment (objecting to the absence of any reference to harm reduction in the CND's political declaration) could potentially form the core of a *'G-26'* treaty reform caucus.

* The NGO community (a growing coalition of human rights, drugs, public health, and development NGOs backed up with a growing number of academic bodies, think tanks and professional bodies) leading on the development of a new public health and human rights discourse in international drug policy at UN level. It would move beyond the polarised legalisation/prohibition debates of the past, instead talking about shared principles and aims, exploring options and potential outcomes, critiquing the failings of the drugs war and explaining in clear practical terms how phased moves towards regulation could bring benefits to individual countries and to the wider global community.

* Serious high level discussion about how the coalition of reform states would redraw the convention system to preserve its beneficial elements, whilst introducing the flexibility for individual or groups of states to explore options for legally regulated production and supply of certain currently prohibited drugs. Such a discussion could be facilitated by the NGO community in conjunction with leading reform states.

* Possible first steps towards more substantive reform are likely to be linked to plant based drugs—cannabis and coca, particularly traditional use.

Further reading

❖ D. Bewley-Taylor, '*Challenging the UN drug control conventions: problems and possibilities*', International Journal of Drug Policy, 2003, Vol. 14, page 171–179

❖ D. Bewley-Taylor, '*Emerging policy contradictions between the United Nations drug control system and the core values of the United Nations*', International Journal of Drug Policy, 2005, Vol.16, pages 423–431

❖ W. McAllister, '*Drug Diplomacy in the Twentieth Century*', Routledge, 2000

❖ D. Barrett, '*Recalibrating the Regime*', IHRA, Human Rights Watch, CHALN, 2008

❖ A. Costa, '*Making drug control "fit for purpose": Building on the UNGASS decade*', UNODC, 2008

❖ Transnational Institute: **www.ungassondrugs.org**

❖ '*Breaking the Impasse; Polarisation and Paralysis in UN Drug Control*', Transnational Institute, Drugs and Conflict Debate Paper 5, 2002

❖ D. Barrett, '*Unique in International Relations? A Comparison of the International Narcotics Control Board and the UN Human Rights Treaty Bodies*', HR2, IHRA, 2008

❖ J. Csete, D. Wolfe, '*Closed to Reason: the International Narcotic Control Board and HIV/AIDS*', Canadian HIV/AIDS Legal Network and International Harm Reduction Development Program (IHRD) of the Open Society Institute, 2007

❖ D. Barrett, M. Novak, '*The United Nations and Drug Policy: Towards a human rights based approach*' (in: '*The diversity of international law: Essays in honour of Kalliopi K Koufa*', pages 449–477), 2009

Appendix 2
Current legal production frameworks for opium, coca, cannabis and pharmaceuticals

The regulated production of psychoactive drugs requires less attention than supply issues. There are already a large range of models in place for regulated production of plant and or pharmaceutical based drugs, from which lessons can be learned. In many cases, given that the same drugs are being considered, production for non-medical use will merely require expansion of existing frameworks. The following consideration of existing legal and regulated production of opium/heroin, coca/cocaine, and cannabis will help demonstrate how this could happen.

Legal production of opium

A significant proportion, almost half,[140] of global opium production is legally produced for processing into opiate based medicines. Any country can cultivate, produce and trade in licit opium, under the

---

140 Licit opium production accounted for more than half of global opium production until the recent bumper harvests in Afghanistan.

auspices of the UN Single Convention on Narcotics Drugs of 1961 and under the supervision and guidance of the INCB. As of 2001 there were eighteen countries that do; of these, four, (China, Korea, India and Japan) cultivate opium poppy for the production of raw opium, although only India exports it. A further fourteen, including the UK, cultivate it for the production of Concentrate of Poppy Straw (CPS), poppy straw, poppy seeds, and alkaloids such as morphine and thebaine. Australia, France, India, Spain and Turkey are the five main exporters of opiates.

Most of these countries use the CPS method whereby the whole plant is cut down—using a combine harvester—after the poppy heads have dried. Once harvested and collected, the pods and stalks are then sent to a factory to be chemically *'washed'*. This process produces CPS which has a higher percentage of active drug content than the more familiar opium gum (also known as opium latex) that is collected by hand, scraped from the growing poppy heads. India is the exception to this rule: it is the only sanctioned exporter of opium gum. Whilst not without problems, this range of scenarios demonstrates that opium production is possible in a range of different environments.

Iran and some Central Asian republics utilise confiscated illicit opium for their domestic medical markets. Mansfield notes that:

> Whilst previously, these countries had been satisfied with using seized opium for their domestic opiate needs, in recent years they have sought to sell seized opiates, or products derived from them internationally. This has caused some concerns amongst 'traditional' producers, such as India and Turkey, as well as the INCB.[141]

Diversion to illicit market

The levels of leakage into the illicit market vary greatly from country to country. There is very little substantiated data concerning this issue;

---

141 D. Mansfield, *'An Analysis of Licit Opium Poppy Cultivation: India and Turkey'*, UK Foreign and Commonwealth Office, 2001.

however some estimates have been produced for India and Turkey, the focus of concerns as the two producing countries which *'converted'* from illicit/traditional production to legal regulated production for medical use.

INDIA

India comes out relatively badly in these estimates due in part to its production method; hand produced opium gum being intrinsically easier to divert into the illicit markets than industrial production of CPS, and in part due to the prevalence of corruption, in turn fuelled by poverty (India being the least developed of the main opium producing countries). Precautions are made to prevent diversions: the Central Bureau of Narcotics (CBN) sets a minimum qualifying yield (MQY) which specifies the number of kilos of opium produced per hectare, and sets a fixed price per kilo. Satellite imagery is issued to estimate the area farmed for licit poppies, and this is compared with exact field measurements taken by CBN officials; since 2007 *'smart cards'* (microchipped identity cards) have been issued to cultivators with personal details of the cultivator and the licensed area; the CBN is also experimenting with CCTV cameras to monitor the collection and weighing of the opium.[142]

The government of India estimates that 10% of total production is diverted into the illicit market, although this is likely to be an underestimate.

TURKEY

Unlike India, Turkey is a producer of CPS, which involves large scale industrial plants and materials, making diversion generally more difficult and less likely. The US State Department claims that there is *'no appreciable illicit drug cultivation in Turkey other than cannabis grown primarily for domestic consumption.'* They go on to state that *'The Turkish Grain Board (TMO) strictly controls licit opium poppy cultivation quite successfully, with no apparent diversion into the illicit market'*.[143] The UNODC says that since *'1974 until now [2003], no seizures of opium derived from Turkish poppies have been reported either in the country or abroad.'*[144]

---

142 US Department of State, *'International Narcotics Control Strategy Report 2008'*.
143 US Department of State, *'International Narcotics Control Strategy Report 2008'*.
144 UNODC Turkey Programme: www.unodc.org/pdf/turkey_programme.pdf.

Production quotas and meeting demand

There are strict controls on the volume of poppy grown in each country annually. Country quotas are set using official estimates of international demand using figures from the past two years' consumption. Whilst India, Turkey, Australia, Spain, and the UK are allowed to grow poppy for the production and export of opiates for pain relief, other countries such as the Czech Republic, Hungary, Japan, Slovakia and Macedonia, for example, are sanctioned to produce opium for their own use. The Senlis Council has stressed that, '*...in 2002, 77% of the world's morphine was consumed by seven rich countries: [the] US, the UK, Italy, Australia, France, Spain and Japan*'. However, according to official figures, '*even in these countries only 24% of moderate to severe pain-relief need was being met*'.[145] There is a real issue here regarding the access of pain relief by developing world countries that do not have a licence to grow poppies.

International legal framework

The international licensing control system seeks to permit and regulate legitimate production and use, while at the same time prevent diversion to the illicit market for non-medical use. National governments deal with the licensing and inspection of cultivation, production, manufacture and trade (including import and export) in the controlled substances whilst being monitored by the International Narcotics Control Board (INCB), which is responsible for ensuring a balance between legitimate production and legitimate requirements.

National governments must provide estimates of requirements for opiates to the INCB for confirmation on an annual basis and they must not exceed these estimates without good reason and the prior knowledge and acceptance of the INCB. The United Nations Office on Drugs and Crime (UNODC) manages the day-to-day monitoring

[145] Quoted in Pierre-Arnaud Chouvy, '*Licensing Afghanistan's opium: Solution or fallacy?*', Asia Times Online, Feb. 1, 2006.

of the situation in each country. The INCB has no actual enforcement powers or punitive sanctions for violations of agreed systems
beyond diplomatic pressure and a process of *'naming and shaming'* in
its annual reports.

Domestic legal framework arrangements

Each of the countries that grows opium poppies for export has its own set of
legal frameworks in order to prevent diversion into the illicit market. Whilst
some are more effective than others, the only significant observations to
come out of reviews of such arrangements are that CPS is considerably less
likely to find its way into the criminal market than raw opium.

United Kingdom

Farmers do not need a licence for poppy growing; however, the police
must be informed of the location. The Home Office confirms this:

> *Although we do not licence growers, we do issue them with a letter
> confirming that we are aware that growing is taking place at their farm
> and detailing the locations. We advise each grower to produce a copy
> of this letter to their local police station in order that they may be aware
> of what is taking place.*

Anyone can grow opium poppies because the process itself is not
controlled by the Misuse of Drugs Act 1971, but any processing of the
plant to extract the opiates is controlled and can only be carried out
under licence.[146] The poppies are grown and then the pharmaceutical
company Macfarlan Smith, who have a monopoly licence to process
opium poppy in the UK, harvest and transport the poppy heads to their
factory for processing. The UK government provides estimates of its
opiate needs to the INCB for confirmation on an annual basis and must
alert the INCB if there is any change to these requirements.[147]

---

146 *'Hampshire—the opium poppy capital of the UK'*, thisiswiltshire.co.uk, 25th February, 2008.
147 UK government's response to the UK Office of Fair Trading review of undertakings by
  Macfarlan Smith Limited, Department of Trade and Industry ruling, Sept. 2006, clause 7.

Tasmania

Licences to grow opium poppies are issued to farmers only after they have been contracted (by one of the licensed companies) to grow and distribute the crop to a licensed manufacturer.[148] Farmers must also have obtained a security clearance from Tasmania Police and provided a detailed plan of the cultivation site. Australia's four-pronged approach to security encompasses industry, government and the rural community, and includes: Property assessments by the Poppy Advisory and Control Board (PACB) field officers along with grower background checks by Tasmania Police at time of licensing; general surveillance and reporting by growers, harvest operators and company field officers, of suspicious activity; investigation of thefts, apprehension and prosecution of offenders and intelligence by a special Tasmania Police Drug Bureau Task Force; and co-ordination of security efforts by the PACB.[149]

India

Central Bureau of Narcotics (CBN) grants licences to eligible farmers in three states—Madhya Pradesh, Rajasthan and Uttar Pradesh. Licences are issued annually for a crop year which commences from 1st October and ends on 30th September of the following year. CBN issues licences to eligible cultivators for licit cultivation in these notified tracts in October every year. The cultivators are required to tender their entire produce to the government. For this purpose, the central government announces a Minimum Qualifying Yield of a certain number of kilos of opium per hectare.[150]

Turkey

The Turkish Grain Board (TMO) allocates licences to farmers once the

148 Poppy and Advisory Control Board (part of the Tasmanian Ministry of Justice) website— 'becoming a grower'.

149 Poppy and Advisory Control Board (part of the Tasmanian Ministry of Justice) website— 'security issues'.

150 India Central Bureau of Narcotics website—www.cbn.nic.in/html/operationscbn.htm.

government has established how much land should be given over to poppy production, and in which provinces and districts it should be grown. The average area cultivated per licensee is about 0.4 hectares, compared to 0.2 hectares in India and about 100 hectares in Australia. In 2001 there were only five provinces in which opium poppies were licitly grown compared to 13 in 1933; the limit was reduced in order to manage the scale of production. The local district office of the TMO monitors the poppy grown in each area to prevent diversion into the illicit market.[151]

Discussion

Expanded production of opium and derived products under the existing framework is clearly both feasible and non-problematic. Even with the economic pressures from illicit demand as they currently exist, the legal production and transit of both raw opium and processed opiate pharmaceutical products currently takes place on a large scale without significant security or diversion issues.

It is likely that the expansion of legally regulated opiate use would initially take place within existing medical prescription models—indeed this process is already underway, albeit slowly. More significant shifts from illicit to licit production (be it via more substantial expansion of prescribing models, or some other appropriate form of licensed sales, see: page 25) would take place incrementally over a number of years allowing for a manageable transition period during which the relevant regulatory and enforcement infrastructure could be developed or expanded, with any emerging challenges responded to.

As this phased process continues demand for illicit products will correspondingly diminish, and with it the economic incentives for diversion or illicit production to occur. This raises potentially significant development issues for Afghanistan which currently produces an

---

151 D. Mansfield, *'An Analysis of Licit Opium Poppy Cultivation: India and Turkey'*, UK Foreign and Commonwealth Office, 2001, page 13.

estimated 93% of the world's illicit opium, contributing over half of its GDP.[152]

FLICKR/SPEEDBOAT
Traditional coca tea

Legal coca cultivation/cocaine production

Both the coca leaf and its active drug content cocaine are subject to strict controls under the 1961 UN Single Convention on Narcotic Drugs, in a similar fashion to opium and opium-based pharmaceuticals.[153] Legal production of both does take place but, compared to the legal production of opium, it is on a much smaller scale and there is much less publicly available information—indeed the whole process is somewhat shrouded in secrecy.

Various low potency coca products, including traditional use of the coca leaf and coca tea, and various other coca preparations including foods and traditional medicines, exist in a legal grey area which remains the subject of ongoing wrangling between the UN drug agencies and Bolivia and Peru.

Coca leaves as a flavouring agent

The 1961 Convention specifically allows for de-cocainised coca leaves to be used as a flavouring agent.[154] The main customer for this flavouring is the eponymous Coca-Cola company, who remain notoriously secretive about their ingredients but do concede that '*de-cocainised flavour essence in the coca leaves*' is used. In the case of Coca-Cola, coca leaves are purchased from South American suppliers by the American conglomerate, Stepan Chemicals Company. In the 1990s they were importing and processing 175 tonnes of coca leaf a year into the US, the only company

---

152 'In Afghanistan, the total export value of opium and heroin being trafficked to neighbouring countries in 2007 is $US 4 billion, an increase of 29% over 2006. That means that opium now accounts for more than half (53%) of the country's licit GDP.' UNODC, '*Afghanistan: Opium Survey 2007*', October 2007, page iii.

153 UN Single Convention on Narcotic Drugs (1961), Articles 23.2.d and 26.

154 UN Single Convention on Narcotic Drugs (1961), Article 27.2.5.

with a Federal licence to do so (issued by the US Drug Enforcement Agency). Separation of the cocaine and flavouring involves a fairly elaborate process in which the leaf is *'ground up, mixed with sawdust, soaked in bicarbonate of soda, percolated with toluene, steam blasted, mixed with powdered Kola nuts, and then pasteurized'*.[155] The de-cocainised product is then shipped to the Coca-Cola company. The volume and destination of the cocaine produced for medical use (at least one tonne of which would be generated from the 175 tonnes of leaf) remaining mysterious, but presumably also administered by the DEA.

A number of smaller product brands also use coca flavouring, many (unlike Coca-Cola) specifically building their marketing around the coca leaf being an ingredient,[156] despite their drinks having no active coca-derived content. These include Red Bull Cola (in the UK), Kdrink, Kokkawine, and Agwa (a coca leaf liqueur).[157] Red Bull Cola state that they source their de-cocainised coca flavourings from Bolivia, Peru and Colombia, and also confirm that the cocaine that is removed from the leaves is passed to relevant pharmaceutical companies for *'medical use'*, and that the various stages of processing are monitored by the health agencies in the relevant countries and authorised by UN agencies.[158]

Cocaine-based pharmaceuticals

There is relatively little information in the public domain about the production and use of pharmaceutical cocaine for medical use. No figures are available regarding the balance of global production (from the de-cocainised leaf based flavourings process), or demand, or whether there is any leakage into the illicit market at any point during the coca/cocaine production process.

In practice, cocaine now has relatively few mainstream medical

155 *'The Legal Importation of Coca Leaf'*, University of Illinois, Class module 9.3, 1999.

156 Unlike Coca-Cola, who would probably do without the ingredient had its inclusion not had trade descriptions implications at the turn of the last century. Pepsi and most other cola brands notably do not include coca.

157 www.redbullcola.com; www.kdrink.com; www.kokkawine.com; www.agwabuzz.com.

158 Transform correspondence with Red Bull, December 2008.

applications.[159] Its former role in anaesthesia has been progressively displaced by newer, more effective synthetically derived alternatives including *Novocaine*, *Lidocaine* and *Xylocaine*. It does however remain as a licensed medicine in many countries including the US, where it is Schedule II (high risk, some medical use, heavily restricted), and in the UK where it can also theoretically be prescribed to dependent users[160] under the same system as more familiar maintenance heroin prescribing models.

Under the 1961 Single Convention, countries that legally produce coca and cocaine are expected to have established an agency to control and oversee the cultivation of coca and production of cocaine. Peru has established such an agency, although whether it functions in the way the conventions intended is moot—the Empresa Nacional de la Coca (ENACO)[161] operates as a state authorised monopoly exporting coca leaves to the US but also produces and promotes a range of coca products including coca tea (*mate de coca*). Peru also manufactures a small amount of raw cocaine to be exported to other countries for the production of medical cocaine.[162] Bolivia similarly also has a national agency to monitor coca production and trade—Bolivian National Direction of Coca Leaf Control (DIGECO).

Coca tea, coca leaf and other coca products

The production, export and distribution of coca tea (*mate de coca*), and coca leaf are viewed by the INCB as illegal under the 1961 Convention, a view forcefully re-emphasised in their 2007 Annual Report[163] (published March 2008). This statement understandably caused outrage in Bolivia and Peru where coca leaf chewing is a long established tradition amongst

---

159 The use of various coca preparations in South America as a traditional medicine in various forms remains widespread.

160 There are, however, few, if any, documented current examples of such prescribing.

161 ENACO website: www.enaco.com.pe.

162 Communication between Transform and the INCB, March 2008.

163 *'The Board again calls on the Governments of Bolivia and Peru to consider amending their national legislation so as to abolish or prohibit activities that are contrary to the 1961 Convention, such as coca leaf chewing and the manufacture of mate de coca (coca tea) and other products containing coca alkaloids for domestic use and export'.* INCB Annual Report 2007 (published March 2008), page 37.

indigenous groups, and mate de coca is consumed widely across all social and economic groups—as freely available as coffee and (conventional) tea. The traditional use of coca leaf has increasingly become a political flashpoint in the international arena, as such long established cultural and traditional indigenous practices have collided with the prerogatives of Western governments determined to stamp out the source of illicit cocaine production that exists in parallel with sources for traditional use.

The historic argument made at UN level for the prohibition of traditional use is essentially that coca is deemed to be an addictive substance; a view traceable back to the World Health Organization Expert Committee on Drug Dependence, which reported in 1952 and 1954, concluding that coca chewing must be considered as some form of cocaine addiction.[164] However, a more recent WHO/United Nations Interregional Crime and Justice Research Institute (UNICRI) study on cocaine use globally found that, *'use of coca leaves appears to have no negative health effects and has positive therapeutic, sacred and social functions for indigenous Andean populations.'*

This exhaustive four year study completed in 1995 was the most comprehensive and in depth study of global coca and cocaine use ever undertaken; it collected data from 22 cities in 19 countries on five continents, analysing coca and cocaine use and its impacts upon communities. In March 1995 WHO/UNICRI announced in a press release that the publication would shortly be forthcoming and summarised some of the key findings. Shortly after this announcement the US representative at the World Health Assembly queried the data and threatened that the US would withdraw its funding to the WHO if they did not disassociate themselves from the report. To date, this report has never been officially published although the relevant sections have subsequently been leaked and made available online.[165]

---

[164] WHO Technical Report Series 57, March 1952, section 62, page 10, and No. 76, March 1954, Section 6, page 10.

[165] WHO/UNICRI, *'The Cocaine Project'* report, 1995, page 16 (for the full document see: www.tdpf.org.uk/WHOleaked.pdf).

The 1961 UN Convention, to which Peru and Bolivia are signatories, says traditional use of coca should be eliminated within 25 years. As the convention came into force in 1964, that deadline passed in 1989. Confusingly, the traditional use of coca was ambiguously addressed in the 1988 Convention, which states that, *'the measures adopted shall respect fundamental human rights and shall take due account of traditional use...'*,[166] and additional concerns have been raised that such prohibitions would violate protections of indigenous cultures enshrined in the UN's Indigenous and Tribal Populations Convention of 1957. The INCB is somewhat isolated in its rigid view of the 1961 Convention; in April 2008 the European Parliament called for the *'safe use'* of some coca-based products (coca tea, etc.) to be explored.[167]

Currently four countries (Bolivia, Peru, Argentina and Colombia) maintain legislation permitting some form of protection of traditional use, to different extents. Bolivia and Peru allow the growing of the leaves for this use, limiting this to a certain amount of hectares. Argentina allows people to carry leaves for traditional chewing, as does Colombia and Chile for their indigenous peoples.

Significant problems exist for the legal and quasi-legal markets in coca-based products in that they struggle to compete with the illegal coca production that supplies the illegal cocaine trade. ENACO said that in 2006 it paid its farmers 1.4 US dollars per kilo of coca leaf, whilst the price on the illicit market is 4 dollars.[168] Interestingly, a shadow market has emerged that pays farmers even higher prices for the coca leaf than cocaine producers; this coca—a gourmet market for the highest quality coca—is used not for cocaine but for the production of traditional use, and bypasses ENACO altogether.

The government of Bolivia is currently led by a former coca grower, Evo Morales, and is actively encouraging the production of traditional coca-

---

166 UN Convention Against Illicit Traffic in Narcotic Drugs and Psychotropic Substances (1988), Article 14, clause 2.

167 *'The role of civil society in drugs policy in the European Union'*, Section 39, 2008.

168 Lasso, *'South America: The business of Legal Coca'*, 2006.

based products such as tea, flour and even toothpaste. In 2006, Morales called for the criminalisation of the coca leaf to end at the UN General Assembly, repeating his call at the 2009 Commission on Narcotic Drugs in a speech that ended with him eating a coca leaf on the podium. In July 2009 the Bolivian proposal to amend the 1961 Convention and remove coca leaf chewing was officially accepted for consideration by ECOSOC.[169]

Discussion

Legal coca production for use in its raw leaf form, lightly processed products, or pharmaceutical cocaine does not present any significant problems in and of itself. Low potency coca products (leaf and tea) do not require any more controls than equivalent products such as coffee, whilst the processing of coca into pharmaceutical cocaine would take place at an industrial level for which any security and product regulation issues would operate within well established models. The key problems in any such system are the ones already seen in coca producing regions: the potentially destabilising economic tensions and pressures created by any remaining parallel illicit market.

Regulating legal production of coca leaf in line with the established fair trade guidelines—price guarantees along with a range other social and environmental protections (for growers of coffee, cocoa, sugar, etc.) would go some way to ameliorating these problems. Furthermore, in a similar fashion to opium and cannabis, such problems would progressively diminish with the shrinking demand for illicit supply, as the global market shifted towards legal regulation of production and supply. Specific trade and development issues might arise during this transition period, including the potential for the UN drug agencies to license production of coca to a limited number of countries (for example limiting it to Andean nations), or for individual states to begin to culti-vate coca for their domestic markets (see: *4.5 Broader social, political and economic impacts*, page 84).

169 Detailed analysis available from the Transnational Institute website www.ungassondrugs.org.

Legal cannabis production

When considering how cannabis production should be regulated in the future, we have a significant body of past experience to draw on. These include legal regulation of cannabis production for a range of purposes (primarily for various medical uses and preparations, but also, to a lesser extent regulation of industrial hemp production and some sacramental/religious uses) in a number of different countries over a number of decades. The challenges and issues raised by these existing models provide a clear indication of how licensed models for cannabis production for non-medical use can evolve as and when the political and legislative environment allows it.

Cannabis holds a unique place within contemporary drug culture and politics, being the most widely used illegal drug globally by an enormous margin,[170] as well as being a plant based drug[171] that can be consumed in its raw herbal form without requiring the significant levels of processing associated with, for example, heroin or cocaine. Regulatory control issues are also complicated by the fact that the plant itself is uncommonly simple to cultivate in a wide range of environmental conditions. The combination of these factors with the enormous and growing demand for the drug (expanding steadily in the West over the past four decades but now showing signs of having flattened off or even falling[172]) means that regulation of cannabis production, supply, and use has presented an impossible challenge from the perspective of prohibition's enforcers; illicit production, supply and availability having more than kept pace with demand.

Quite aside from the insurmountable and evidently never ending enforcement nightmare this presents (the most recent figures available are from 2003 when it was estimated that the illicit retail cannabis

---

170 The UNODC estimates that about 160 million people use cannabis annually—3.8% of the global population aged between 15 and 64. '*UNODC Annual Report 2008*', page 10.

171 It contains a number of active substances, the two key ones being THC and CBD.

172 '*The production and consumption of cannabis levelled off for the first time in the last decade*'— '*UNODC Annual Report 2008*', page 10.

market was worth about \$113 billion[173]) the almost total lack of market regulation means that large scale production is not only in the hands of unlicensed growers, untaxed and unmonitored for environmental impacts, but the product itself is not subject to any controls, so strength/potency[174] cannot be gauged or controlled and there is no ability for the relevant agencies to intervene on problems with quality controls such as contamination.[175]

Legal cannabis production for medical use

The most useful contemporary model for production of cannabis is for its medical uses, in both processed and herbal form.

Processed medical cannabis-based products

The UK based company GW Pharmaceuticals produces a product—Sativex—which is the world's first pharmaceutical prescription medical product (standardised in composition, formulation and dose) derived from the cannabis plant. It differs from some similar synthetic products (see below) in that it is derived directly from the botanical source, and contains two active ingredients from the cannabis plant, THC and CBD (there are a range of different formulations). The cultivation of the cannabis plant used to make this product operates under a special licence granted by the UK Home Office (as permitted under section 7 of the Misuse of Drugs Act 1971). These licences allow the company to research and develop cannabinoid prescription medications such as Sativex. According to GW Pharmaceuticals the cannabis plants are grown under *'computer-controlled conditions in secure glasshouses'* which allow *'Strict Standard Operating Procedures'* to be followed *'to ensure non-contamination by chemicals, infestation or fungal growth, consistency of*

173 *'UNODC World Drug Report 2005'*, page 127.

174 Including relative potency of THC and CBD, that can influence the prevalence of some of the negative side effects of cannabis intoxication including psychotic symptoms/episodes.

175 There have been a number of examples of cannabis being contaminated with various substances. A 2007 case documented street cannabis being bulked up (by weight) with lead particulates leading to a significant number of serious lead poisonings, in the New England Journal of Medicine, *'Lead Poisoning Due to Adulterated Marijuana'*, April 10, 2008.

content, methods of harvest, drying, primary extraction, storage and onward consignment'. The farming takes place at a secret location in the South of England.

It is interesting to note that there are currently two other prescription drugs based on compounds found in the cannabis plant. The first is dronabinol (marketed as Marinol) that contains the main active drug component of cannabis: tetrahydrocannabinol (THC), but which is produced entirely synthetically. In 1986 in the US, Marinol was moved from Schedule 1 (no therapeutic uses—the schedule in which cannabis/ marijuana remains) to Schedule 2, allowing it to be prescribed in oil based gel-cap form, albeit under very strict conditions. In 1991 the UN Commission on Narcotic Drugs similarly moved THC and its stereoiso- mers (chemical variants) from the UN Schedule I (no therapeutic value) to Schedule 2 (of limited therapeutic value), freeing Marinol from the very tight restrictions imposed by Article 7 of the 1971 UN Convention on Psychotropic Substances. In the US during 1999 Marinol was then moved again into US Schedule 3.[176] Three years later, at its 33rd meeting in 2002, the World Health Organization's Expert Committee on Drug Dependence recommended transferring THC to UN Schedule IV of the 1971 Convention (the least tightly-controlled schedule), citing its medical uses and low abuse potential. The expert committee then reconsid- ered this recommendation in 2006[177] recommending a move only to UN Schedule 3. They notably found that *'Dronabinol is the main active principle of cannabis and has similar effects on mood, perception and the cardiovascular system'.*[178]

The other cannabinoid based drug is Nabilone, which is synthetically produced and mimics the effects of THC, apparently with reduced side effects, notably the euphoria associated with THC.

176 According to a timeline produced by J. Gettman—this move was 'in response to a petition filed by the manufacturer on February 3, 1995'. Online here: www.drugscience.org/lib/bib_tl.

177 *'WHO Expert Committee on Drug Dependence. Thirty fourth report',* page 10 (2.1.1).

178 There have been some high level discussions in some countries about attempting to reschedule cannabis from its current UN Schedule 1, notably parliamentary debates in the Netherlands in early 2008 around addressing the ambiguous legal status of the countries cannabis policy. Such a move has yet to be seriously discussed at the UN level in the Commission for Narcotic Drugs.

Unprocessed or herbal form medical cannabis products

The use of herbal cannabis for a range of medical uses is well established and has substantial backing from a broad spectrum of the scientific and medical community.[179] It remains controversial in the medical world because, unlike almost all other licensed drugs, it is consumed in its raw herbal form (seen as a *'messy'* cocktail of active substances), because it is frequently smoked (although it can be used with a vaporiser or eaten in variety of preparations), and because it has not been through the standardised rigours of other potential prescription drugs.

There are also ethical issues around potential side effects, not least pleasurable ones, and concerns about diversion to non-medical use. None the less, provision of medical herbal cannabis does exist in various forms and provides some useful indications for how potential non-medical production models may operate in the future.

US legal production

In the American political arena, medical cannabis production, supply and use is arguably more controversial (than, for example, use of St. John's Wort as an anti-depressant, that lacks any parallel non-medical/recreational uses), as the issue has become inexorably entwined with the wider political and cultural discourse about non-medical cannabis use and legislation. None the less, the widely reported efficacy of herbal cannabis relative to standard prescribed drugs for a large number of individuals with chronic illnesses, who do not fit the bill as stereotyped drug users, has forced the issue. Thirteen states now allow the use of medical cannabis—they are Alaska, California, Colorado, Hawaii, Maine, Maryland, Montana, Nevada, New Mexico, Oregon, Rhode Island, Vermont, and Washington.

There is an ongoing conflict between state and federal governments.

---

179 *'Supporting Research into the Therapeutic Role of Marijuana: A Position Paper of the American College of Physicians'*, January 2008.

Individual states exercising what they view as their right to allow medical cannabis production, supply and use, have repeatedly clashed with the federal government's insistence that cannabis has no therapeutic value as a Schedule 1 drug under US law. As a result, there have been a series of unpleasant enforcement incidents, with federal police closing down medical production and dispensaries that were officially sanctioned by state governments. Bizarrely, the US federal government itself produces and supplies medical cannabis for users, who receive monthly consignments of pre-rolled joints.

At the time of writing there are only four surviving participants in the Compassionate Investigational New Drug (IND) programme run by the Food and Drug Administration (FDA). These patients have been provided with medical cannabis for between 11 and 27 years. The cannabis is grown at the University of Mississippi under the auspices of the National Institute on Drug Abuse (NIDA). Material is shipped to the Research Triangle Institute in North Carolina where it is chopped and rolled on modified tobacco cigarette machines, then stored partially dehydrated and frozen. The joints are distributed to each of the users on a monthly basis.

Legal cannabis production in Canada

A similar scenario has played out in Canada where, in 2001, medical use of cannabis was legalised in restricted circumstances through the Canadian Department of Health's Medical Marihuana Access Division.[180] According to their Marihuana Medical Access Regulations, individuals can get licences to produce their own supply of cannabis, or a licence can be given to another designated individual to grow on their behalf. In 2000 Canada's department of health, Health Canada, contracted Prairie Plant Systems, on behalf of the federal government, to grow cannabis in an underground mine at Flin Flon Manitoba for research purposes, and in 2003 to distribute to the expanding number of medical users in the

180 Health Canada website: www.hc-sc.gc.ca/dhp-mps/marihuana/supply-approvis/prairie_e.

government programme.[181] Health Canada notes that:[182]

> Under the terms of the original five-year contract PPS signed with
> Health Canada, the company:
>
> * Set up and operated a marihuana growing, processing, fabrica-
>   tion and storage establishment;
> * Conducted laboratory testing and quality control of marihuana
>   throughout the product's life cycle;
> * Fabricated, packaged, labelled and stored marihuana material;
> * Conformed with the requirements of the Controlled Drugs
>   and Substances Act, including stringent security and physical
>   measures;
> * Distributed marihuana to patients and researchers.

Along with the estimated 600 users of the Prairie Plant Systems
cannabis there are over 11,000 users of 'compassion clubs' in Canada.[183]
These clubs act as medical cannabis dispensaries, supplying cannabis
for therapeutic use upon a valid recommendation or confirmation of
diagnosis from a licensed health care practitioner.[184] Whilst the Senate
Special Committee on Illegal Drugs[185] and other government bodies have
recommended that these organisations be licensed and legally recognised, currently they are operating without legal sanction.

These groups are currently self-regulated. They set clearly defined
standards, including demands that a variety of strains be offered

---

181 Health Canada's Medical Marihuana Access Division website:
www.hc-sc.gc.ca/dhp-mps/marihuana/index_e.

182 There have been concerns raised about the quality of cannabis produced at Flin Flon;
see: 'Open Letter of Concern for the Health and Safety of Canada's Medicinal Cannabis
Community', Canadians for Safe Access.

183 Lucas, 'Regulating compassion: an overview of Canada's federal medical cannabis policy and
practice', Harm Reduction Journal 2008, 5:5, page 9.

184 Capler, Lucas, 'Guidelines for Community-Based Distribution of Medical Cannabis in Canada',
May 2006, page 4.

185 'Measures should be taken to support and encourage the development of alternative practices,
such as the establishment of compassion clubs'—Nolin, Kenny, 'Cannabis: our position for a
Canadian public policy. Report of the Senate Special Committee on Illegal Drugs', Summary
Report, September 2002, page 20.

and that cultivation must be carried out without the use of chemical fertilisers—which potentially lead to contamination with heavy metals—pesticides or fungicides. Cultivators must also protect the cannabis from yeasts, moulds, mildews and fungi. The clubs undertake their own independent testing of contaminants and potency.

Cannabis production in the Netherlands

Cannabis production in the Netherlands exists in an peculiarly ambiguous legal grey area created by the collision of the country's policy of *de facto* decriminalisation—for personal use and licensed sales (through the *'coffee shop'* system—see: page 26)—and their UN drug treaty commitments that enforce a strict prohibition on production. Whilst small scale cultivation for personal use is tolerated (as elsewhere in Europe), larger scale production or importation for supplying the coffee shops is not, and has been the subject of an increasing enforcement effort over the last few years. In previous decades Dutch criminal enterprises were more closely involved in European and international cannabis trafficking but an enforcement push in the late 1990s dismantled much of this activity and coincided with the expansion of domestic illicit production, both in the Netherlands and elsewhere.

Domestic production of herbal cannabis now constitutes 75–80% of coffee shop sales, and whilst it is unregulated in terms of strength and contamination it is considered to be of generally good quality. There is no reliable data available, however, a substantial proportion of domestic Dutch production is still thought to be for export to neighbouring countries. The exported cannabis is rumoured to be of lower quality, and thus not acceptable in the coffee shops—it is supplied as vacuum sealed product more easily bulked up with non-cannabis materials. Most hash/resin form cannabis in the coffee shops is still imported from Morocco, through established illicit routes.

Traditional cannabis use in India

Cannabis (also known as ganja or bhang in India) has been used in India for many centuries. It is associated with one of the main Hindu gods—Shiva—and is also used openly during traditional annual festivals, most commonly the spring festival of Holi. Until India became a signatory of the 1961 UN drug convention, the sale of bhang was controlled by the government who managed the drugs

A 'Government Authorised' traditional cannabis shop in Jaisalmer, India, 2006

trade through licensed sales and the collection of taxes. Government bhang shops were, and in some cases still are, prevalent throughout large parts of India.

Under the 1961 Single Convention they, like many other countries who had what was described as *'traditional use'* of scheduled drugs, were obliged to end the use of such substances within 25 years. In a similar fashion to the traditional use of the coca leaf in the Andes this has, perhaps unsurprisingly, not happened (the 25 year window perhaps being a signal that it was never likely to either). There are still *'official'* government bhang shops in some cities such as Varanasi and Puri (and others across Rajasthan), and it is still widely used during religious festivals, as well as on a more regular basis by a small number of holy men or Sadhus. Recreational use of bhang by Western tourists is not uncommon. Production of the bhang, which is relatively low potency and most commonly eaten or in a beverage, is essentially unregulated, operating much like production of herbs and spices.

Small scale domestic production for personal use

As has been discussed above, cannabis is relatively simple for individual users to grow and prepare for use in their own gardens, or own homes using freely available lighting and grow systems. These cannot be legally restricted or controlled as they have a wide range of other legitimate uses. Given this reality, small scale domestic production has become increasingly popular and widespread, supported by a burgeoning industry in growing guides and literature, technology and paraphernalia. This development has been facilitated by the difficulty in legislating against the distribution of cannabis seeds, which do not themselves contain the active drugs.[186]

Some countries have put in place regulations for domestic production for personal medical use. Canada—as discussed above—is a good example. Under the Medical Marihuana Access Division regulations it allows the issuing of *'personal use production licenses'*, which allow small scale production (using a formula to determine a limited number of plants/yields) under strict licensing criteria.

In Spain the policies of decriminalisation of personal possession and use of cannabis also cover the right for individuals to grow a limited number of plants for their own personal use.

Discussion

The licensed production of cannabis, on a medium to large scale, for medical use in a number of countries, demonstrates clearly how it is possible for such production to take place in a way that addresses both security concerns and quality control issues. Production for non-medical use would presumably not need to meet quite such exacting standards on either front. For example, going as far as growing in an underground mine would seem somewhat excessive.

186 Seeds are, for example, legal in the UK and Canada, but not in the USA.

Legitimate concerns about diversion to illegal markets could be addressed through appropriate licensing of growers and suppliers, combined with effective enforcement where violations of licensing conditions were identified. Clearly the economic incentive to divert to illegal markets would progressively diminish as legal production expanded and undermined the profits currently on offer to illegal suppliers. As with opium and coca products discussed above, the expansion of legal production would be incremental over a number of years, allowing for a manageable transition and the evolution of an effective regulatory infrastructure in response to any emerging issues and challenges.

It seems likely that—if a legal, retail supply was available—home growing for personal use would become an increasingly minority pursuit, rather like home brewing of wine or beer: the preserve of a small group of hobbyists and cannabis connoisseurs. In practical terms it would be near impossible to license non-commercial small scale production, even if some of the product was circulated amongst friends. Home tobacco growing in the UK is theoretically subject to customs duty but is virtually non-existent. Basic guidelines could be made publicly available and limits could be placed on how much production was allowed for any individual but experience with such schemes in Europe suggests they are hard to enforce and often ignored by police and growers alike. A licensing model might become appropriate for small to medium sized cannabis clubs or societies of growers who share supply/exchange on a non-profit basis, so that age and quality controls could be put in place, and some degree of accountability could be established.